DONATO CRETI

The exhibition "Donato Creti: Melancholy and Perfection" held at The Metropolitan Museum of Art, New York, from October 27, 1998 through January 31, 1999, has been organized by the Musei Civici d'Arte Antica, Bologna with the cooperation and assistance of the Italian Ministry of Foreign Affairs, the Italian Institute of Culture, New York and the Italian Ambassador to the United States, as part of the initiatives for Bologna European City of Culture for the year 2000.

Under the Patronage of the President of the Italian Republic.
With the support of the Italian President of the Council of Ministers, the Minister of Foreign Affairs and the Minister of Cultural Heritage.
With the participation of the Committee for Bologna European City of Culture for the year 2000.

This exhibition and the publication of the English and Italian editions of this catalogue are made possible by Saima Servizi Spa of the Saima Avandero Group.

DONATO CRETI

Melancholy and Perfection

Edited by Eugenio Riccòmini and Carla Bernardini
in cooperation with Keith Christiansen

OLIVARES

The Musei Civici d'Arte Antica, Bologna
wish to thank:

Museo Civico Archeologico, Bologna,
with special thanks to Cristiana Govi Morigi,
Paola Giovetti and Gioia Meconcelli
Biblioteca Comunale dell'Archiginnasio,
Bologna, with special thanks to Pierangelo
Bellettini and Valeria Roncuzzi
Servizio di Rete Civica Iperbole of the Comune
di Bologna
Biblioteca Comunale, San Giovanni in Persiceto
Biblioteca Universitaria, Bologna,
with special thanks to Biancastella Antonino
and Rita Giordano
Soprintendenza ai Beni Artistici e Storici,
Bologna, with special thanks to
Andrea Emiliani, Anna Colombi Ferretti,
Daniela Bertocci, Giampiero Cammarota,
Marzia Faietti and Corinna Giudici
Archivio di Stato, Bologna
Musée du Louvre, with special thanks
to Stèphane Loire
Graphische Sammlung Albertina, Wien
with special thanks to Konrad Oberhuber,
Renate Antoniou and Veronika Birke
University Art Museum of SUNY at Binghamton,
with special thanks to Jacqueline Hogan
Christ Church Picture Gallery, Oxford

and also:
Mario Armellini, Emanuela Bagattoni,
Wanda Bergamini, Donatella Biagi Maino,
Francesca Melli, Antonella Nasini,
Giovanna Perini and David S. Tabbat

and especially
Federica Olivares, for her active
and intelligent involvement

Donato Creti: Melancholy and Perfection
Catalogue © 1998, Musei Civici
d'Arte Antica di Bologna
Texts © 1998 Eugenio Riccòmini
and Carla Bernardini

Editorial Coordination
Francesca Melli
Antonella Nasini

Translation
David S. Tabbat

Graphic Design
Andrea Lancellotti

ISBN 88-85982-42-5
© 1998 MCF srl - Edizioni Olivares
via Pietro Mascagni, 7
I - 20122 Milano
Phone: +39 2 7600 1753
Fax: +39 2 7600 2579
E-mail: olivares@tin.it

Table of Contents

The Metropolitan Museum of Art is extremely pleased to host the exhibition "Donato Creti: Melancholy and Perfection" and, in doing so, to celebrate Bologna as European City of Culture in the year 2000. To lovers of Italian art Bologna is identified with the names of the seventeenth-century painters Ludovico and Annibale Carracci, Guido Reni, Domenichino, Guercino and Giuseppe Maria Crespi. The Metropolitan celebrated their great moment in the history of European art in the memorable "Age of Correggio and the Carracci" exhibition held in 1987. Donato Creti was not included, since his work is of the eighteenth century rather than the seventeenth.

There are few pleasures in life as rewarding as the discovery of an obscure master and this, in effect, is what this focused exhibition promises to the American public. That the works in it should be the artist's single greatest achievement—a cycle of paintings undertaken over a period of years for his most enthusiastic patron—makes the pleasure an undiluted one. For this opportunity I would like to thank Walter Vitali, Mayor of Bologna, and Roberto Grandi, Deputy Mayor Cultural for their support of this project; Eugenio Riccòmini, Appointed Director of the Musei Civici d'Arte Antica in Bologna, who first proposed the exhibition; Carla Bernardini, Curator of the Collezioni Comunali d'Arte - Musei Civici d'Arte Antica in Bologna; Giordano Gasparini, Director of the Department of Culture in Bologna; the Ministero degli Affari Esteri; and Gioacchino Lanza Tomasi, Director of the Italian Cultural Institute in New York, who has worked tirelessly to assure that the exhibition would take place. We are extremely grateful to the generosity of Saima Servizi Spa of the Saima Avandero Group, whose support has made the exhibition possible.

Philippe de Montebello
Director of The Metropolitan Museum of Art

This exhibition of works by Donato Creti is the first of many events which will mark the year 2000: a year during which Bologna will figure among the European Cities of Culture. This makes it all the more significant that these paintings—exquisite manifestations of Bolognese art and tradition—are crossing the Atlantic as messengers of our culture.

I should like to thank, first and foremost, Philippe de Montebello, Director of the Metropolitan Museum, for his role in making this important event possible. Without his support, this exhibition could never have taken place. I also thank Gioacchino Lanza Tomasi, Director of the Italian Cultural Institute of New York, for his help, and Alvise di Canossa for his support. Lastly, I wish to express my gratitude, and that of the city I represent, to all the numerous individuals, companies, and official organizations whose involvement has been fundamental to the success of this enterprise and particularly to Filippo Sassoli de Bianchi.

The selection of Bologna as a European City of Culture is a challenge for all of us. As well as calling upon us to live up to our great artistic tradition, it urgently demands that we remain a vital presence in today's world and in that future which is about to be symbolized by the birth of a new millennium.

Here, then, is a precious chance to give a renewed impetus both to our city's creativity and to its capacity for bringing its creations to the world's attention. As stimulating as it is demanding, this is an opportunity for working together towards a renewed conception of the value of culture in all its forms, here in an Italy which is at long last discovering, in the beauty of its own history and past glories, a vital stimulus and resource for the years to come.

Walter Vitali
Mayor of Bologna

The Donato Creti exhibition at The Metropolitan Museum of Art offers an opportunity to draw the American public's attention afresh to the ongoing importance of artistic creation as a distinguishing feature of Italian civilization. Given the intense concentration of nineteenth-and twentieth century America's great collectors upon the most important Italian masters of the Renaissance, it may seem superfluous to speak of the attention devoted to Italian art by American cultural institutions. By this same token, however, the outlook of today's average American museum-goer still reflects a deeply rooted hierarchy of values closely linked to the standards of judgement expressed by the sixteenth-century Tuscan writer Vasari. "Oh, yet another Italian painter?" Thus, perhaps, may be summed up the widespread climate of indifference surrounding new discoveries and the deeper exploration of less-familiar aspects of Italian art, especially since the decrease in that reverently respectful, practically automatic recognition of Italian art's central role which went essentially unchallenged from the fourteenth century down to the eighteen-hundreds. To win an audience here in America for Italian painting of the nineteenth and twentieth centuries—let alone such lesser-known eighteenth-century art as that of Creti—is a truly arduous undertaking, one calling for time, dedication, and tenacity. In this context, the present show is a step in the right direction, for it calls attention to the dense and complex intellectual ramifications underlying our Italian culture.

If the event is taking place in so prestigious a setting as the Metropolitan Museum, this is owing, first and foremost, to the passionate love of Italian art of both Philippe de Montebello and Keith Christiansen. Both men belong to that breed of scholars from abroad whose admiration for our culture also manifests itself in true friendship for their Italian interlocutors. I think that every Italian museum director or art historian who has ever met Keith Christiansen has felt an unexpected sense of relief upon discovering his enthusiasm, and has drawn comfort from dealing with a scholar whose evident respect for their professionalism and commitment is not always matched at home. Sigmund Freud has described the relationship between the artist and society as a special case of the cycle of production and consumption. The price the artist pays is isolation; and yet, through his work, the artist ultimately has a deeper impact upon the development of society than do those who work "within" it in a more direct sense.
I am grateful to all our American and Bolognese friends for the manifestation of friendship that this event embodies.

Gioacchino Lanza Tomasi
Director, the Italian Cultural Institute
New York

Art lovers who pride themselves on their knowledge of Italian painting may be forgiven their inability to conjure up an image at the mention of the name Donato Creti. He has, after all, been an object of neglect for more than two centuries, a neglect that was underserved but perhaps inevitable, given the critical opprobrium his famous seventeenth-century predecessors Annibale and Ludovico Carracci, Domenichino and Guido Reni suffered at the hands of Victorian critics such as John Ruskin.

The heady, moralistic language that characterized nineteenth-century critical writing about Baroque painting left little room to admire or even to condemn the work of Creti, whose art seemed removed from the social and aesthetic issues of nineteenth-century society.

Today, when Baroque painting is no longer an object of disdain and Bolognese painting has become a field of intense study, Creti still awaits the recognition that is his due. In many ways, his is an art of contradictions. It can seem quintessentially of its time and place - an exquisite and rarified homage to Guido Reni and the classical-idealist tradition of Bolognese painting. But whereas the strength of that tradition lay in its large scale fresco cycles and monumental altarpieces, Creti excelled on a more modest scale. His frescoed ceiling in the Palazzo Pepoli in Bologna demonstrates that he was capable of undertaking ambitious tasks, but he was not at home painting the grandiose universe we associate with Tiepolo. Similarly, his altarpieces are noble but can lack the seductive charm and delicacy of his easel paintings.

The Italian critic Roberto Longhi certainly had Creti's preference for smaller, less formal, more intimately pitched paintings in mind when, in 1935, he christened the artist the Bolognese Watteau - "questo Watteau bolognese." Longhi's epithet is at once suggestive and misleading. It may come to mind in front of paintings such as Creti's *Shepherds in a Landscape* (Art Gallery, Belfast) and his sparkling *Dance of Nymphs* (Palazzo Venezia, Rome). It may even be extended, albeit somewhat eccentrically, to the enchanting series of small pictures in the Vatican showing figures in landscapes with, in the heavens above, astronomically observed depictions of the planets and the moon.

However, Creti strove to evoke the classical poetic ideal of Arcadia, not the aristocratic one of the fête galante. His real arena was allegories and mythologies, elegantly acted out by pristinely drawn figures, whose intense blue and red garments shimmer in a crepuscular Venetian light.

There is no denying that the difficulty in categorizing Creti's art has added to his obscurity. His finest paintings have the airiness and delicacy of touch of a Rococo painter but aspire to a formal purity and an ideal of perfect beauty that, in many respects, looks ahead to Neoclassical painting. Yet Creti shared none of the Neoclassicists' fascination with antiquarian studies or their obsession with ancient precedent; poetic invention and the capriccio were Creti's forte, though as often as not applied to subjects with a mythological or biblical theme. Francesco Algarotti, art advisor to the king of Poland, proposed commissioning from Creti something "graceful and light", while the Irish impresario and entrepreneur Owen McSwiny turned to Creti for the figures in his projected suite of canvases designed as imaginary memorials to illustrious British men. These kinds of limited tasks were the result of applying conventional expectations to Creti's work, a mistake made by many critics and art historians today.

It fell to Creti's two greatest patrons to give him commissions suited to his special gifts. Cardinal Ruffo, who spent hours observing Creti at work, commissioned not only the capriccioso Dance of Nymphs, for which he awarded the artist the title Cavaliere dello speron d'oro, but also exotic biblical subjects about King Solomon. Marcantonio Sbaraglia commissioned Creti to produce a cycle of pictures that combined classical mythology, allegory, and poetic conceits. The paintings were viewed by Creti's biographer Gian Pietro Zanotti as his finest work and a summation of his art. Sbaraglia bequeathed the paintings to the city of Bologna in 1744, and they remained on view in the Palazzo Pubblico until sometime in the nineteenth century, when they were put in storage. Presumed lost, they were rediscovered only in 1933 by Guido Zucchini and included in the groundbreaking exhibition of eighteenth-century Bolognese painting held in 1935, an event that symbolically marks the reintroduction of Creti into the history of Italian art. After the exhibition the paintings were installed in the handsome gallery in the Palazzo Pubblico where visitors to the city can still see them today. It is Sbaraglia's cycle of paintings that has been lent to the Metropolitan Museum, providing an American audience an opportunity to become acquainted with this marvelously gifted artist. For this occasion Eugenio Riccòmini has written what is for me the finest critical appreciation of Creti - one that, together with Renato Roli's groundbreaking monograph, will constitute the starting point for anyone seeking to understand the motivations behind his work.

Confronting the paintings of an unheralded Old Master for the first time is not the simple task it may at first seem. We bring with us prejudices and expectations that may have nothing whatever to do with his art. It is worth recalling that, when Henry James visited Bologna in 1873, he was so under the thrall of Ruskin that he confessed - rather proudly - to "scowling most unmercifully at Guido and Domenichino" (Italian Hours).

The only reason Creti was not scowled at was that by then he was virtually unknown: indeed, had James consulted his Baedeker, he would not have found Creti in its index. This exhibition will, I hope, put Creti back in the public eye and serve not only to enchant Museum visitors but also to inspire students to take up the study of eighteenth-century Italian painting - a field that, in America, remains grossly misunderstood and undervalued. When Goethe visited Bologna in 1786, he was puzzled by the many works he saw by unfamiliar artists, yet he made the wise observation that, "it is the same in art as in life. The deeper one penetrates, the broader grow the views" (Italian Journey). A pity Goethe's stay in the city was so brief and hurried that it did not include a visit to the Palazzo Pubblico. My deep thanks to Eugenio Riccòmini and to Gioacchino Lanza Tomasi for making Creti's work available to those who may never have visited that wonderful city.

Keith Christiansen
Jayne Wrightsman Curator
of Italian Paintings
The Metropolitan Museum
of Art, New York

DONATO CRETI PITTORE E CAVALIERE ACCADEMICO CLEM ✠

Donato Creti
Melancholy and Perfection

Donato Creti was nearing the end of his long life and career when he turned his hand to the two large canvases intended for the Sanctuary of the Madonna di San Luca, the place of worship dearest to the hearts of his fellow townspeople. High on a hill overlooking Bologna, the church was like a visible sign of Heaven's protection of the city; and so, in fact, it still appears today when, from the highway or the train, the traveler catches a glimpse of a long portico winding up through the greenery until it reaches the bare, oval-shaped mass of the church itself.

When Creti began those two pictures, however, the building was still awaiting completion after twenty years of construction. For the artist, the commission represented a reward, a public acknowledg ment of his merits. In the archives we come upon documents telling us how he was "the only man in Italy worthy enough" to take on the noble and prestigious task; "the only Painter capable of adding, through his labors, further lustre to a place"[1] so eminent, so much in the eye of townspeople and foreigners alike. In short, the assignment must have been very satisfying to him. It meant, to be sure, glory at home, but also on the far side of the Alps and beyond the sea: all the more so since Creti was, at that very moment, already at work on a painting depicting a subject drawn from antiquity for the king of Spain and two others for the duc de Noailles,[2] maréchal of France.

As well as bringing the painter a considerable sense of satisfaction, the Bolognese commission might thus have occasioned him legitimate pleasure; even a certain smug pride. And yet, as we draw closer to one of these large altarpieces, we notice that Creti has written on it something more than just his signature and the statement that he painted it at the age of seventy-four. He has appended an unusual note, addressed to the viewer, in which he describes himself as "having always lived in a state of illness, and continuously sleepless for thirty-six years, being reduced to a state of delirium, unable to find rest by night or by day. Gentle viewer, reflect, and pity me."[3]

But just what, today, are we meant to reflect on? And why should we feel sorry for Creti? To us, his paintings seem utterly crystalline visions, closely paralleling the limpid, Classicizing poetry advocated by the influential Bolognese Arcadian literary taste of Creti's day. These pictures also strike our modern eye as the eighteenth century's most disciplined and faithful continuation of that dream of an ethereal beauty, unsullied by the vulgarity of everyday life,

Portrait of Donato Creti
(engraving from
Giovan Pietro Zanotti's
*Storia dell'Accademia
Clementina*, 1739).

which had taken shape in the mind of Guido Reni; this dream was passed on to others in the busy tranquillity of Guido's Bolognese studio, where artists studied every imaginable perfection of draftsmanship and painting.

That is how things appear to us today. And the impression grows even stronger when our gaze turns from those labored altarpieces, weary with the artist's old age, to the heroes and nymphs and centaurs and putti who - bathed in a light as diaphanous as any aquarium's - dance their way through the series of painstakingly thought-out paintings originally executed more than twenty years earlier as decorations for the study of a Bolognese gentleman. After being hung in the antechamber of the high civic official known as the Gonfaloniere, these pictures were installed in a sumptuous gallery in the town hall, where they can still be seen today.[4] And yet, if we may believe that autograph inscription on the altarpiece (couched in a language at once humble and proud, and seemingly calculated to forestall any possible criticism), then it would appear that, over twenty years earlier, Creti was already plagued by insomnia and delirium and was, as he says, incapable of ever attaining peace or repose.

Marcantonio
Franceschini
Death of Abel, 1723
oil on canvas,
Pinacoteca Nazionale,
Bologna.

We moderns, steeped in every sort of romantic and bohemian aesthetic, are used to equating a life of desperation with sublimity in art: Caravaggio the murderer, van Gogh the suicide and so on. Still, we can't fail to be struck by the contrast between, on the one hand, the self-pity inscribed alongside the signature and, on the other, the graceful, exquisitely academic perfection of these depictions of Greek and Latin myths.[5] Nonetheless, we must bear in mind that Creti's anguish, his obsessive depression, was not an imaginary illness invented to ward off the judgment of critics and peers. There exists, for example, a legal document drawn up in 1720, in which he is described as *mentis veluti impos et a se ipso distractus*, that is, out of his mind and, in modern terminology, schizophrenic;[6] admittedly, this document is the work of a party hostile to Creti and concerns a disagreement over the attribution and appraisal of a group of old paintings. But we also have the many pages dedicated to him by the abbé Giampietro Zanotti, secretary of the Accademia Clementina. Before being printed in 1739, the text, written in the most limpid Italian, was read and approved by a committee of academy members, including Creti himself. Zanotti's biography mentions at the outset that the artist was "oppressed by sadness, and weighed down with melancholy," "assailed by sinister and troubling phantasms," to the point that he "lost both reason and sanity, as well as tranquillity and repose."[7] The text closes (after a long description of the very paintings in this exhibition) with a return to its opening theme, making a final reference to the "sad and sinister melancholia" that had made the artist's entire life such a misery. One might mention that Zanotti, in the handwritten marginal notes he added to his own printed copy of the volume, flatly calls Creti "mad" at least five or six times.

Carlo Cignani
Flora, 1681
oil on canvas,
Galleria Estense, Modena.

Well, then? What are we to make of these pictures, which have reminded modern scholars of Poussin, Albani, even Watteau? Must we scrutinize them more carefully, in order to descry

hidden traces of madness? Or was Zanotti mistaken, despite his knowing the artist well and seeing him nearly every day?

Donato Creti had already passed his fortieth year when, about 1713, Marcantonio Collina Sbaraglia engaged him to paint the stories of Achilles, along with four Virtues and some monochrome overdoors; afterwards, the same patron would also add the commission for the two largest mythologies, so that work on the project as a whole was destined to continue until after 1721.[8] The artist had begun his career as a child prodigy, of precocious intelligence and seductively attractive appearance. Throughout the city he was referred to as the little boy ("ragazzino")[9] and he enjoyed the favor of count Alessandro Fava, a sharp-eyed connoisseur, an amateur painter and a patron of the arts. Creti's pictures were sought out by all the aristocratic families of Bologna and by collectors from elsewhere as well. At the time he received the initial commission from Marcantonio Sbaraglia, he had just painted, beneath the loggia of the town's ancient university, a monument commemorating Giovan Girolamo Sbaraglia, a famous professor of philosophy and anatomy and a fierce opponent of the more modern thought of Marcello Malpighi.[10] Creti had played a role in the foundation of the Accademia

Clementina and had twice served as its director. In short, the painter did not lack for success and recognition.

And yet it is not inconceivable that it was precisely the creation of the Accademia that drove Creti down a sort of blind alley and ultimately threatened his fragile equilibrium. As the official teaching establishment in the city, the academy was not simply a place for learning but also for inculcating rules and making inevitable comparisons between participating artists. Thus, the Accademia Clementina could not be anything other than an expression of the most widely accepted cultural positions. In its teachings, as in the practice of the artists belonging to it, the Accademia could aspire only to a balanced, moderate compromise between tradition and innovation; and naturally, it would tend to favor consolidation of the glorious local tradition over any sort of break with the past, however timid. (Zanotti, secretary of the Accademia right from its foundation, expressed his great diffidence toward innovations, "which turn everything upside-down" and can lead artists down "frequently dangerous paths").[11] Above all, the academic environment, then as now, was suspicious of those exceptional individuals who did not hew to the middle path. Creti was an outstanding example of such a personality and was well aware of it.

As it happens, there was another exceptionally inventive painter at work in Bologna at that time. This was Giuseppe Maria Crespi and it is no accident that in his manuscript glosses Zanotti also calls Crespi a "madman" and even a "beast." It is a remarkable coincidence meriting some reflection that in those years the two most singular and serious painters in Italy (and perhaps in all of Europe, if we except Watteau) were living in the city of the Carracci, of Guido Reni and of Guercino. Both were heirs to that city's rich tradition; both at once faithful and recalcitrant toward it; stubbornly insisting upon their diversity and excellence (even if they manifested this insistence in different - indeed, in opposite - ways). Both were contrary, in life as in art, to the tranquil, somewhat anemic academic correctness of Marcantonio Franceschini, a faithful disciple of Carlo Cignani, who had himself been the first head of the academy, nominated for life. For Franceschini, who was of an older generation than Crespi and Creti, the abbé Zanotti has only praise: he lauds the painter's "excellence in art" as well as his "angelic manners, goodness and forthrightness".[12]

It was Franceschini's clear, limpid style, solidly rooted in tradition yet more pleasing to the taste of the period because of its diffused luminosity, that seemed to Zanotti and his contemporaries the model to be emulated. His art was equally distant from the concrete earthiness of Crespi's, with its plebeian vulgarities and Dutch-like curiosity regarding optical

Lorenzo Pasinelli
Martyrdom of Saint Ursula
1680-1685
oil on canvas,
Pinacoteca Nazionale,
Bologna.

14

effects and everyday life, and from the extreme refinement of Creti's, with its emphasis on sharp, crisp drawing and unrealistic, gelid colors.

It was precisely this very sort of middling taste - or, as they used to call it back then, good taste - that Creti refused to settle for, finding it too restrictive. It is easy to imagine how limited he thought the eminently reasonable advice that, in those very years, between 1708 and 1715, Ludovico Antonio Muratori was advocating for the use of poets and artists in his Riflessioni sopra il buon gusto. There we find recommended a style of "noble seriousness and gravity" informed by "that decorum which one ought to seek in all things, being loved and looked for by souls truly noble and possessed of perfect taste."[13] Muratori had the chance to see a good number of pictures by Franceschini, both in Bologna, a city he visited frequently, and in his native Modena where, for example, the Bolognese painter had frescoed the "hall of honor" of the ducal palace in 1696, as well as the apse of the church at the prestigious noblemen's college of San Carlo in 1701. Even more important, Muratori read with approval the verses of several Bolognese poets, all of them friends of the abbé Zanotti, who aspired to the role of "reformers of fine literature in Italy". They were horrified by any kind of overwrought subtlety or Baroque complication and desirous of steering poetic practice back into the safe and quiet haven of Petrarchan tradition: a haven, in short, located on the shores of Arcadia.[14] The poet Foscolo was later to say of these men: "They were more correct than animated; and, wishing to cleanse poetry of the turgid excesses of the previous century, they fell into the opposite defect, bleeding it dry".[15] The best of them, the mathematician and astronomer Eustachio Manfredi, published his own verses in 1713, just as Creti was girding himself to begin our mythological paintings. Creti must have had at least a slight acquaintance with Manfredi's poetry, if only because of the duties imposed by friendship. Barely two years earlier, Manfredi, as director of the astronomical observatory at the Institute of the Sciences, had provided the painter with helpful suggestions regarding some delicious little scenes of planetary observations, afterwards given to Pope Clement XI and now among the gems of the Vatican collections.[16]

Who knows? Creti may even have liked those verses, written in perfect classicizing prosody, but rather bloodless and lacking in color. When it came to his own painting, however, he was much more demanding. So far as Classicism was concerned, Creti had never even set foot in Rome and he made no bones about the fact that he cared neither for the work of Domenichino nor for that of Raphael.[17]

What he did like - or rather, what he absolutely adored - was that "certain heavenly and

Marcantonio Franceschini
Summer, 1716
oil on canvas,
Pinacoteca Nazionale,
Bologna.

divine concept" always manifest in Guido Reni's perfect canvases. In those "most choice" works ("which sometimes went beyond what was required," warned the cautious Zanotti) Creti discovered "the flower of beauty and grace".[18] Not for nothing had he passed his days, ever since childhood, copying Guido's drawings and the prints by Cantarini, which are their faithful translation. Not for nothing had he chosen to study with Lorenzo Pasinelli, who, as Cantarini's most careful and intelligent follower, could fairly claim to be the most legitimate of all heirs to the Reni tradition.

So it was with the great and burdensome spectre of Guido Reni that Creti was competing. He had indeed issued a bold challenge. If he was to win the contest, he would have to best his matchless and legendary predecessor on the latter's own terms: flawless draftsmanship; compositions that, for all their ingenuity, managed to look simple and spontaneous; a manner of coloring likewise entirely artificial, untainted by any vulgar realism, and yet so internally coherent as to seem believable and convincing.

Zanotti was quick to take note of this contest of Creti's with Reni (and, even more, with himself). Here is his commentary on two of the pictures in the present exhibition: "In this figure of Mercury, and in the other one representing Paris, one sees clearly that Creti had in mind the style of Guido's *Samson*."[19] In a sort of prophecy of what was, in fact, going to happen in just a few years' time, Zanotti adds that these pictures by Creti "might not inappropriately be hung alongside this last-named painting;" i.e., in those same public rooms of the Gonfaloniere where Guido's *Samson Victorious* had long been an object of admiration, devoutly visited by every foreigner passing through the city. It may, perhaps, have been Zanotti's comparison that, four years later, induced the Bolognese Senate, which had accepted Creti's pictures as a gift, to hang them in the rooms of the Gonfaloniere along with the *Samson*.[20]

Still Zanotti's observations strike us nowadays as pretty banal; all the more so since in Bolognese painting one finds oneself constantly surrounded by all-too-familiar figures and poses, imitations of imitations in a non-stop display of déjà vu.

In the present case, in fact, we are not faced with imitation in the usual sense, but with emulation, which is quite another matter. Creti has here made a wager for very high stakes indeed: he is betting that he can surpass Guido's models by creating compositions, figures, and settings of even more flawless beauty. Given that perfect beauty is not of this world, Creti was driving himself into ever-more-rarefied territory, further and further removed from any direct contact with reality and with Nature. This is to say that he was moving in the exact opposite direction from that taken by Giuseppe Maria Crespi, who finished his important series of the *Sacraments*, now in Dresden, in 1712: paintings where the point of departure is the observation of the ways light really falls in the aisle of a church. Unlike Crespi, Creti may never even have glanced at the world out of his window. He wanted his idea of beauty to pass

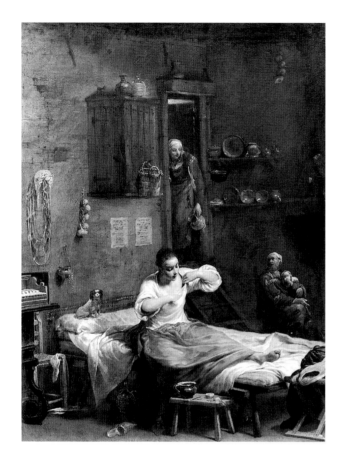 

Giuseppe Maria Crespi
The Flea
1720-1725, oil on canvas,
Musée du Louvre, Paris.

Giuseppe Maria Crespi
The Scullery-Maid
about 1725, oil on canvas,
Galleria degli Uffizi, Florence.

intact from his mind to the canvas, with no interference. Of course, perfect beauty must always be unique: no variations, no alterations, forever identical to itself. This is why Creti is forever recycling the same types of heads. Sometimes he repeats them in lines; sometimes he poses them symmetrically, as mirror images of themselves; but he never alters their appearance. Already, some years earlier, in the fresco of *Alexander Cutting the Gordian Knot* in Palazzo Pepoli, Bologna, he had contrapuntally repeated, six times, the same head of a warrior of antiquity.

That head also recurs here, in the canvas showing *Achilles Dragging the Body of Hector*, where it does duty for the two warriors on the left, as well as for the hero himself. One might add that, in this last picture, he applies this same principle, with maniacal yet superb inventiveness, to the two horse heads facing in opposite directions yet identical.[21]

For us, today, it is certainly difficult to read the exquisite beauty of such paintings as anything more than academic. We find it hard to view that lovingly finished back of a nymph in the episode depicting *The Infant Achilles Entrusted to Chiron* without its putting us in mind of Ingres, Hayez, or even Couture. Academic practice, however, always involves a mediation between, on the one hand, the museum, with its canonical works, and, on the

Giuseppe Maria Crespi
Confession
1710-1712, oil on canvas,
Staatliche Kunstsammlungen,
Dresden.

Lorenzo Pasinelli
Peace
1670-1680, oil on canvas,
Pinacoteca Nazionale,
Bologna.

other, the real-life models offered the artist in the studio or classroom. But here there is no trace of any such mediation. The settings, for example, have nothing at all to do with normal visual experience: neither the imagined "ideal city" - as spiky with spires and columns and domes as any Baroque stage set - that here does duty as Troy; nor the blade-sharp profile of those imagined mountains, immersed in the bluish light of some deep seabed. All we can see here is the anxious pursuit of perfection.

The same may be said of the coloring. There are no adequate names for those two carefully calibrated hues, related yet different, somewhere between ash-gray and turtledove, the color observable in the garment of the allegorical figure of *Humility*.

This is painting that takes us down the road leading to abstraction: to art as an activity concerned only with itself. One of the countless manifestations of this orientation in these pictures is the absence of any precise iconographic significance in the monochrome figures (half of whom are shown in thrall to Somnus or Sleep, that ancient divinity whose absence Creti felt so intensely in his own life); they are treated exclusively as models of absolute perfection, to the point where some of them already look as though they could date from the time of Canova and Fuseli.

Another instance is the obsessively studied handling of the draperies in the four Virtues; this drapery is the true subject of the pictures. For Zanotti, the "excessive copiousness of folds"[22] was, among the flaws of contemporary taste, an error of excess. But in these pictures excess is the point. We have already noted that Creti felt himself involved in a competition; and when you're competing, you go for broke, pushing to excess, however heavy the cost in terms of lost sleep and psychological stress. Zanotti obviously thought that this price was too high: "For his profession's sake, he studies ceaselessly, sighs, suffers, and falls prey to obsessions, such is his longing for perfection and glory; nor does he tire of ceaselessly laboring over his pictures." In a manuscript addition, appended to his biography of the painter immediately after the latter's death, Zanotti notes in astonishment: "The desire to surpass everybody, including the masters of the past, utterly destroyed him; and this desire was combined with another, equally intense need for praise and immortality."[23] As noted by his modern biographer Renato Roli, this obsession amounted to a "narcissism from which there was no way out."[24]

But perhaps Creti did find a kind of way out after all through the creation of the subtly diseased perfection we have before our eyes today. These pictures are pervaded by an anxious beauty that has been pursued to the last detail and, in the end, captured. If Creti was seeking some sort of immortality, he may, in the end, have found it; and the attainment of such a goal was well worth the loss of tranquillity, repose, and sleep.

Eugenio Riccòmini

19

Notes

1. This praise is found in the manuscript *Notizie intorno alle due Cappelle grandi laterali del nuoro Tempio della Madonna di San Luca, et alli due Quadri del Cav. Donato Creti in dette collocati* (ms. 89, Biblioteca Universitaria di Bologna) and in *Riflessioni intorno a' Quadri, ed agli ornati degli Altari della Chiesa di S. Luca* of 1740; the complete texts have been published by Renato Roli on pp. 73-74 of his volume Donato Creti, Milan, 1967, a work of fundamental importance for our knowledge of the artist.

2. The picture for the king of Spain represented *Alexander Giving His Concubine Campaspe to the Painter Apelles*. Roli, op. cit., pp. 81-82, quotes a letter dated October 11, 1735 from Creti to the architect Filippo Juvarra, in which the artist announces that he has begun work on the canvas, intended for the throne room at La Granja in Segovia; but the work was still unfinished as of 1740. In that same year of 1740, Creti was also at work on two paintings for the duc de Noailles, maréchal of France; now lost, they depicted *Alexander and his Physician* and *Alexander Cutting the Gordian Knot*. The very beautiful bozzetto, or oil sketch, for the first of these subjects, has turned up in a private collection; cf. M. Riccòmini, "*A rediscovered bozzetto by Donato Creti*," in The Burlington Magazine, June 1989, p. 420.

3. The inscription is located in the lower half of the altarpiece showing *The Madonna and Saints*, adjacent to several small figures in whom the artist has portrayed himself and his family; cf. Roli, op. cit., p. 70.

4. The story of how these paintings were commissioned by Marcantonio Collina Sbaraglia, and subsequently donated to the Bolognese Senate, is told by Carla Bernardini in the present catalogue. The Gonfaloniere was the head of the civic administration; the position, not altogether unlike that of a modern-day mayor, was assigned by rotation to members of the various noble families whose representatives made up the Senate. Although the latter body's scope of political action was restricted by the presence of the Cardinal Legate - a sort of governor sent by the Pope, who was himself the sovereign and head of state - true administrative power in the city was nonetheless vested in the Senate. The Gonfaloniere was largely confined to a ceremonial role, given that he remained in office for barely two months. The Gonfaloniere's rooms, where Creti's pictures were hung, are still the offices of the mayor of Bologna today.

5. The episodes involving Achilles shown in these works are not derived exclusively or directly from Homer's *Iliad*. It seems more likely that the patron for the commission drew upon the *Achilleïs* of the Roman poet Statius, where we find, for instance, the episode of the infant Achilles immersion in the waters of the Styx in an effort to ensure him immortality.

6. This annotation was tracked down by G. Perini; cf. "*Donato Creti inconsueto*" in *Arte a Bologna*, Bollettino dei Musei civici d'arte antica, no. 1, 1990, p. 62. Following a manuscript by the Florentine Gabburri, the same article also a cites a conversation between Creti and another Bolognese painter (surely Giuseppe Maria Crespi, recently returned to Bologna from Florence), in the course of which Creti makes some quite harsh strictures upon Florentine painting.

7. G.P. Zanotti, *Storia dell'Accademia Clementina*, Bologna, 1739, vol. III, p. 99. Founded in 1710, the Academy, named for the reigning Pope Clement XI, was made up of forty artists. Its principal task was instruction in the fine arts by means of regular courses, at the end of which the most deserving students were awarded prizes. From 1711 on, the Academy was housed in the sixteenth-century Palazzo Poggi, sharing it with the newly formed Istituto delle Scienze, which was equipped with classrooms and laboratories for the teaching of mathematics and the sciences, and even with an up-to-date astronomical observatory. At a time of decadence in the history of the very ancient University of Bologna, these two new organizations, working side by side, were intended as proofs of a true renaissance of scholarship and the arts, in accordance with the model offered by the royal academies of France and Great Britain. Both the Accademia Clementina and the Istituto delle Scienze were disbanded during the Napoleonic period, being replaced respectively by the Accademia di Belle Arti and by various branches of the university; these successor institutions still possess a large part of their predecessors' original didactic materials and artistic and scientific holdings. The newly established State University was installed in the same Palazzo Poggi formerly occupied by its predecessors, and is still housed there today. A recent study of the Academy is A.W.A. Boschloo, *L'Accademia Clementina e la preoccupazione del passato*, Bologna, 1989.

8. In October of 1721, the two largest canvasses in the series (*Mercury and Juno* and *Mercury and Paris*) were still undergoing preparation prior to painting. This fact, along with much other detailed information, is to be found in R. Roli's essay on the entire group shown here: "*Il Creti a Palazzo: il lascito Collina Sbaraglia al Senato di Bologna (1744)*" in *Arte a Bologna*, Bollettino dei musei civici d'arte antica, no. 1, 1990, pp. 49 et seqq.

9. The information comes from Luigi Crespi, *Felsina. Vite de' pittori bolognesi*, vol. III, Rome, 1769, p. 257.

10. Giovan Girolamo Sbaraglia (1614-1709), who taught anatomy, medicine, and philosophy at the University of Bologna for fully forty years, published studies of the nature of nerves and glands. Still, his name has come down in the annals of medicine solely on account of his polemical opposition to the more advanced experimental methodology propounded, first and foremost, by Marcello Malpighi (1628-1694). The latter was a brilliant researcher who discovered the capillaries and the functional mechanisms of the lungs; a member of the Royal Society of London, he was also the Pope's chief physician.

11. G.P. Zanotti, op. cit., vol. IV, p. 348.

12. G.P. Zanotti, op. cit., vol. I, p. 247.

13. The Modenese abbé Ludovico Antonio Muratori (1652-1750) is remembered as one of the founders of a modern historiography based on a precise, philologically skilled knowledge of the archival sources. He was the author of works of fundamental importance to which historians still turn today, particularly for the study of medieval Italian history. But Muratori was also interested in poetics (*Della perfetta poesia italiana*, 1706) and aesthetic problems: various passages of his *Riflessioni sopra il buon gusto* offer critical propositions such as the one cited in the present essay, here drawn from the Venetian edition of 1759, vol. II, chap. IX.

14. There exists by now an extensive bibliography regarding Bolognese Arcadian poetry: see above all the recent *La Colonia Renia*, M. Saccenti, ed., Modena, 1988. This study includes, in vol. III, pp. 361 et seqq., an article by F. Montefusco Bignozzi, "*La Colonia Renia e le arti figurative*," which clarifies the relationship between poetry and painting.

15. This comment by the great poet of the Neo-Classical period appears in a note to his short *Storia del sonetto italiano*, written in 1816 during his period of exile in England; now available in Ugo Foscolo, *Opere*, vol. X, p. 427. The poet Giacomo Leopardi expresses a similar opinion regarding the Arcadian poetry of Eustachio Manfredi: "It is nothing more than clear and facile and well-bred and elegant, nowhere revealing the slightest hint of power." The quotation is from G. Leopardi, *Zibaldone*, vol. I, p. 118.

16. The eight pictures, representing observations of the Sun, Moon, Mercury, Venus, Mars, Jupiter, Saturn, and a comet, were ordered as a gift to Pope Clement XI by the general Count Luigi Ferdinando Marsigli, a man of both war and science, the moving spirit and true founder of the Istituto delle Scienze and the Accademia Clementina. Many of the astronomical instruments shown in the paintings are still preserved today in the Specola or observatory. This structure, contemporary with the pictures, was built in 1725 by the architect Giuseppe Antonio Torri; it looms like some ancient keep atop the sixteenth-century mass of the Palazzo Poggi.

17. "He finds Raphael intolerable. He hasn't a penny's worth of regard for Albani, and doesn't much like Domenichino." G.P. Zanotti appended this manuscript annotation to p. 122 of his personal copy, previously mentioned, of the printed edition of his own *Storia dell'Accademia Clementina*.

18. G.P. Zanotti, op. cit., vol. I, p. 25.

19. G.P. Zanotti, op. cit., vol. III, p. 113. Guido Reni's masterpiece, painted around 1611 for the Zambeccari family, was donated to the Senate of Bologna in 1684 by Cardinal Boncompagni. It remained on display in the Gonfaloniere's rooms until 1796, when it passed to the Accademia di Belle Arti. The picture now hangs in the Pinacoteca Nazionale in Bologna.

20. In its session of November 10, 1744, the Bolognese Senate voted to accept this entire group of pictures by Creti as a gift, deciding that the works would be displayed in the chambers of the Gonfaloniere; cf. Roli, op. cit. 1990, p. 56, no. 32.

21. This unusual iconographic invention also appears in ancient Roman art, although most infrequently. It occurs, for example, on the verso of a gold coin of the Emperor Augustus, on the Arch of Galerius at Salonika, and on a sarcophagus of the Imperial period; this last is illustrated in K. Schauenberg, *Stadtrömische Eroten-Sarkophage*, III, Zirkusrennen, Berlin, 1995, cat. no. 117, p. 90. In Italian painting or painting done in Italy, it is found in Domenichino's fresco of 1615 representing *The Chariot of the Sun* in Palazzo Costaguti in Rome; in one of Poussin's earliest Roman works, *Joshua's Battle against the Amalekites* of around 1630, now in the Hermitage in Saint Petersburg; and in a drawing by the Florentine artist Giovanni di San Giovanni, likewise dating from about 1630: the *Allegory of Wisdom* recently published, of which mention has already been made, in the catalogue *Disegni antichi della raccolta Franchi*, Bologna, 1998, p. 94, fig. 43.

22. G.P. Zanotti, op. cit., vol. III, p. 349.

23. As in other instances mentioned above, Zanotti added these hand-written observations to his own printed copy of his *Storia dell'Accademia Clementina*. The comment cited here occurs in a concluding note added to p. 122.

24. Roli, op. cit. 1967, p. 38.

I

Donato Creti and the Quest for Perfection

Edited by
Carla Bernardini

Of all the Bolognese painters of his time, Donato Creti—"the Guido Reni of the eighteenth century"—is the one whose early development was most closely bound up with the extraordinary cultural ferment that characterized Bologna during the late seventeenth and early eighteenth centuries. His formative years saw the gradual birth of the Accademia Clementina, the city's first and only public art academy, and slightly preceded the creation in 1714 of the Institute of Science, an important event in the history of the Enlightenment. The Accademia was open to scientific innovation, experimentation, and an approach to teaching marked by a cosmopolitan spirit and the complementary application of various disciplines. In this it differed from the University of Bologna, which remained reluctant to accept new ideas from outside Italy.

During this same period, Bologna also experienced a renewal in the aesthetic and literary fields that soon brought it up to date both with the reforming impulses originating in France and with the Arcadian sensibility originating in Rome.

In the sciences, as in literature and the arts, this new cultural climate had been promoted by several private academies. Bologna's particular historical and cultural situation thus meant that Creti had the opportunity of entering into contact with certain key figures and artistic circles and to make their taste and culture his own.[1] We owe our current knowledge of the artist to a number of important studies. Since the appearance in 1967 of the monograph by the historian and critic Renato Roli, other publications, many by Roli himself, have expanded the artist's oeuvre and provided detailed information about certain of its aspects. Especially the recognition of a vast corpus of drawings is proving indispensable to the clarification of his complex chronology.[2] Note should also be made of the recent reconstruction of the artist's early years, based upon little concrete data and more precise understanding of his relationship with the art of the Veneto and, in particu-

Annibale Carracci
Medea
1584, fresco,
Palazzo Fava, Bologna.

lar, of that of Paolo Veronese (1528 - 1588).[3]

Donato Creti was born in Cremona in 1671. His father Giuseppe was "Bolognese, a painter of illusionistic architectural settings, but with a poor reputation," as we are told by Creti's first biographer Zanotti. Donato went to live in Bologna at the age of two. There, while still a young boy, he received his earliest training in the art of drawing, for which he revealed a natural predisposition, and soon developed an interest in the prints of Guido Reni (1575 - 1642) and Simone Cantarini (1612 - 1648). His precocious gifts gained him admission to the famous classes in drawing from the nude model held in the house of the painter Lorenzo Pasinelli attended by the city's most promising young painters and sculptors, including Giovan Gioseffo dal Sole and the sculptor Giuseppe Maria Mazza.[4] The "foundations of Donato Creti's idealistic motivations" have been identified as a Classicism softened by elements drawn from Venetian painting, along with the "vision of an Arcadia inhabited by the living memory of much great painting."[5] One of Creti's classmates in Pasinelli's studio was the artist and man of letters Giovan Pietro Zanotti, the ideologue and moving spirit behind the Bolognese academy, who was to devote many pages to Creti in his *Storia dell'Accademia Clementina*.[6] Like his brother, the man of letters Francesco Maria Zanotti, Giovan Pietro was destined to play an important part in the propagation of the Classicizing aesthetic typical of the Bolognese artistic circles of the period.[7]

Pasinelli's classes were also attended by Pietro Ercole Fava, the son of Count Alessandro Fava; the latter became the young Creti's patron and protector. Palazzo Fava was a natural setting for the formation of young artists, since its rooms had been frescoed by the Carracci and their school (i.e. the famous cycle of the *Stories of the Argonauts* and the *Quest for the Golden Fleece* and of *Jason and Medea*, as well as several episodes drawn from the *Aeneid*, and the *Story of Europa*).[8] Creti's earliest commissions from Count Fava produced a large number of paintings, and even more drawings.[9] As early as 1693, Creti's fame as a draftsman had reached the ear of Johann Adam of Liechtenstein, a patron of Marco Antonio Franceschini.[10]

According to Zanotti, both Creti and his teacher Pasinelli bitterly regretted that the young artist's talent and refined taste had not been further enriched by a thorough course of general studies; this lack was, according to Zanotti, the source of Creti's sense of inadequacy and psychological distress. Zanotti says that Creti "began to suffer such fits of melancholy as to give rise to serious fears for his sanity." He adds that the artist "was well aware that up to that time he had not studied as he knew one ought to do, but only in accordance with his pure natural instincts: something much praised in the young, and which in them appears sufficient, but which is not so in adults," since "however intense and effective natural feeling may be, it can produce no finished work unless it be regulated and cleansed." This biographical passage, which refers to a moment when the painter was turning away from Classical forms and his earliest models as a result of his discovery of the painting of Giovanni Antonio Burrini and Sebastiano Ricci,[11] implies a conception of artistic talent inseparable from long study and the mastery of academic draftsmanship.

Palazzo Fava, that cultural crossroads,[12] was also the seat of the Accademia letteraria degli Accesi, the membership of which included all the leading literary and scientific figures of early eighteenth-century Bologna: the Marchese Orsi, famous for his contribution to the bitter literary polemics regarding the relationship between French taste and Italian traditions;[13] Eustachio Manfredi, a scientist and man of letters, the future astronomer of the Institute of Science; and the great Bolognese poet Pier Jacopo Martello, the most important protagonist of a classicizing reform of literature based on a return to Greek and Roman culture and a crucial figure in determining Creti's artistic orientation. Many of these same personalities meet in the Colonia Renia, the Bolognese branch of the Accademia dell'Arcadia in Rome, the leading force in the reform of literary aesthetics in a reaction against the reigning Baroque taste. It was at Palazzo Fava that the decision was made in 1706 to open a public academy of painting, with Creti among the signers of the request submitted to the Bolognese Senate.[14] The need for such an institution had been felt for years; it was to become a means of breaking the enduring link of painting with the ancient guild system and of emphasizing it as a liberal art, of institutionalizing artistic training, and of opening a dialogue with the illustrious academies already extant in Florence and Rome. The project was taken up a few years later by Count Luigi Ferdinando Marsili when he promoted the creation of the Accademia Clementina in his palace in Strada San Mamolo in Bologna; he named the new academy after Pope Clement XI Albani, who had supported the project (Bologna forming, at the time, part of the Papal States).[15] By the time the new institution was solemnly inaugurated in January of 1711 in the presence of all the civic and ecclesiastical authorities, Creti was a very well established artist. He had tried his hand at the "grand" Classical manner in his *Philip of Macedon Placating the Anger of Alexander*, formerly in Palazzo Fava and now in the National Gallery in Washington. He had subsequently demonstrated his strict formal control and refined elegance in *An Old Woman Telling the Story of Psyche to a Girl*, a beautiful canvas not devoid of genre-like hints of everyday life of a sort rare in Creti. In *Hagar and the Angel*, he had revealed an atmospheric range of nocturnal tonalities.[16] Ever since his youth, Creti had also accepted the challenge of working in fresco. In the *Hercules and Cerberus* in Palazzo Fava recently attributed to him,[17] Carraccesque elements still abound. Since the decorative frescoes he executed around the year 1700 in the castle at Novellara have been lost, his most important surviving works in this medium are the three ceilings painted in Palazzo Pepoli with the help of the quadraturista [painter of illusionistic architecture] Marcantonio Chiarini. Creti was to give up working in fresco after the *Sbaraglia memorial* painted in 1713, probably on account of the technical difficulties he had encountered in this last-named work as a result of his use of oil paints on the wall.

In Palazzo Pepoli, the site of Creti's most significant surviving frescoes, the most challenging comparison his work had to withstand was with the "rustic" Arcadia of Giuseppe Maria Crespi, embodied just a few years earlier in the ceilings with the *Feast of the Gods* and the *Seasons*, works entirely innocent of abstract allegorical elements or moralizing programs. Nothing could be farther removed from the refined, lucid representation

Ercole Lelli
Portrait of Giovan Pietro Zanotti
(engraving from Giovan Pietro Zanotti's *Storia dell'Accademia Clementina*, 1739).

D. Fratta and G. Benedetti
Portrait of Luigi Ferdinando Marsili
(engraving from Giovan Pietro Zanotti's *Storia dell'Accademia Clementina*, 1739).

*Laboratories and rooms of the
Istituto delle Scienze, Palazzo Poggi,
with the School of drawing from
the nude of the Accademia Clementina
miniature of 1739
(executed on the occasion of the visit
to Bologna of the Prince Frederic Christian
of Poland, Archivio di Stato, Bologna,
Insignia degli Anziani, vol. XIII, c. 140).*

Donato Creti
The Dance of the Nymphs
about 1724, oil on canvas,
Museo di Palazzo Venezia,
Rome.

*The School of Drawing
from the Nude*
(frontispiece of G.P. Zanotti's
*Storia dell'Accademia
Clementina*, 1739).

Donato Creti
*Allegorical Tombs of Locke,
Boyle and Sydenham*
1729, oil on canvas,
Pinacoteca Nazionale, Bologna.

of Antique themes and the fantastic spacial constructs of Creti's ceilings.[18] In this first decade of the new century, Creti's patrons had been almost entirely noble (generally linked to the Senatorial aristocracy), and prevalently interested in secular themes taken from ancient history.

The century's second decade opened for Creti with two commissions from the refined cultural circles frequented by the artist. The first was the altarpiece for the chapel of the Accademia degli Argonauti in the College of Nobles at Santa Lucia, where young aristocrats were educated; the picture (now in the City Art Collections of Bologna) shows *Saint Francis Saverio Invoking the Virgin's Protection for Sailors*.[19] The second commission was for the eight little canvases now in the Vatican Museums showing *Landscapes with Observations of the Planets*, ordered by Count Marsili to help convince the Pope of the necessity of building an astronomical observatory in Bologna. In these works, objective observation of scientific instruments and planets—the work of a specialized miniaturist collaborator—coexists with an idyllic spirit that reveals Creti's study of the sixteenth-century frescoes by Niccolò dell'Abate in Palazzo Poggi, friezes with figures and landscapes that evoke the poetry and spirit of Reinassance "courtly" culture.[20] Palazzo Poggi became the new seat of the Institute of Science, and thus housed the astronomical observatory, construction of which had been promoted by Marsili and supported by Pope Clement XI. With the Institute's occupation of its new quarters, there came to fruition a good part of the Enlightenment dream of creating a structure intended specifically for a type of teaching based on direct experience and facilitated both by an adequate array of scientific instruments and by the didactic models Marsili made available for each of the disciplines ("So as to teach with the eyes," he said, and not with words"). The Accademia Clementina, too, which was associated with the Institute of Science, likewise became a place where teaching depended not upon lessons in theory, but upon the use of models, with particular emphasis on drawing (which was studied jointly by painters and sculptors), architecture, and stage design. Artists practiced drawing from the collection of plaster casts, sculptures, and wooden models donated by Marsili himself, which provided the materials for a training in imitation of form still based upon the theoretical formulations current a century earlier.

One such formulation, regarding "universal good taste" based upon a "regulated mixture" of styles, had been theorized by Carlo Cesare Malvasia in his *Felsina Pittrice* of 1678, a work of fundamental importance for Bolognese artistic historiography.[21] Malvasia's book was still drawn upon by mid-eighteenth-century theoreticians such as Giovan Pietro Zanotti and his brother Francesco Maria, the poet and man of letters, both of whom wrote theoretical texts that help shed light on Creti and his work. Giovan Pietro was the author of *Avvertimenti per lo Incam-minamento di un giovane alla pittura* [Advice for Setting a Youth on the Road to Painting] of 1756; Francesco Maria, of the *Arte poetica*. In these works, academic norms and a not overstrict adherence to visible reality form the general context for an aesthetic aiming at the occupation of a "praiseworthy middle ground" ["lodevole mediocrità"]. Ample scope is nonetheless left for individual creativity, both because the artist's "eyes [have been] well indoctrinated in matters concerning good rules" and are therefore to be trusted, and because "grace" is theorized to be a pure and gratuitous gift of Nature, and is thus unteachable. In a return to the viewpoint attributed by the historiographic tradition to the Carracci, "The work of imitation was not accomplished through servile subjugation to a precise style, but by forming a new extract of various manners."[22] Such theories also left room for the French-inspired subtlety and intellectual lucidity that had made their way into Bolognese culture, and which Zanotti saw embodied in Creti.

Creti's art, having "blossomed in a key of serene, suavely Arcadian fantasy," arrives in his late works at "an inviolate formal craftsmanship marking something close to the unsurpassable limit of any further perfectibility."[23]

The varied types of expression Creti experimented with during the years when he was working for Marco Antonio Collina Sbaraglia constituted the basis for his subsequent creative work, which was to focus for many years on easel paintings representing secular subjects; only in his final years was he systematically to turn his hand to altarpieces. By about 1720 he had achieved on a quasi monumental scale a highly individual translation of the "grace" generally regarded as appropriate to pictures of lesser dimensions, his paintings of *Jacob's Struggle with the Angel* comes close to being a formal dance, while *Jacob's Ladder* is a reworking of the art of

Ludovico Carracci (1555 - 1619) as filtered through Guido Reni's refinement—Creti then moved on to the grandiose conception underlying his two pictures now in the museum in Clermont-Ferrand (*Solomon and the Queen of Sheba* and *Solomon Censing the Idols*). These canvases were painted for Cardinal Tommaso Ruffo, Papal Legate at Bologna in the middle years of the century's second decade, and brought the artist the title of Knight of the Order of the Golden Spur at a time when he had already been named head of the Accademia Clementina. After such works, the road leading the grandiose style of the allegorical tombs of illustrious English personages commissioned by Owen McSwiny (an eighteenth-century amateur) was open. In those pictures landscape, figures, an archaeologizing taste, and stage-set-like architectural settings coexist in extraordinary harmony, leaving ample scope for a dreamily poetic vein where the calm of Arcady lapses into melancholy.[24]

During the artist's full maturity and last years, the streak of formal purism he had long cultivated in secular works found expression in altarpieces. These works reveal an underlying connection with Guido Reni's nobility of form and refined color harmonies—intensified, however, by a brilliant palette reminiscent of the late paintings of Guercino's (1591 - 1666) late altarpieces. Especially in the two altarpieces Creti carried out in 1737 and 1740 for the church of San Pietro, the theatricality of the altar setting is dissolved by a narrative and sentimental tendency that places these works among the masterpieces of European religious painting. This narrative slant is also responsible for the introduction of curious details, as in the altarpiece of the *Madonna and St. Ignatius* (1737), in which there appears a witty inscription that it is Creti himself we see in the background, dressed *all'antica* and pointing

Donato Creti
Pastoral Scene
about 1730, oil on canvas,
Pinacoteca Nazionale,
Bologna.

Donato
Creti
Battle of Jacob and the Angel
about 1720, oil on canvas,
Casa del Clero, Bologna.

to the Specola, the astronomical observatory at Palazzo Poggi.[25]

Creti belongs to the same classicizing breed of artists as Carlo Cignani (1628 - 1719), the seventeenth century's worthiest heir to the tradition of Classicism, and Marco Antonio Franceschini (1648 - 1729). Nonetheless, his artistic and emotional situation was unique, as distant from the grace and sensibility of Cignani's brand of Classicism as from Franceschini's purism, with its academically approved use of effective gestures. Ercole Graziani was Creti's pupil and immediate follower, but he failed to perpetuate his master's most original vein. If Creti had no imitators or professed followers, this is because his painting did not embody a style that could constitute a basis for further development in the codified realm of Bolognese Classicism, it was therefore unsuitable as an object of study or imitation.

Creti's painting expresses, instead, a particular way of feeling and of reacting to inherited tradition, and of expressing oneself through the language of such a tradition; indeed, his work is a case of that language's being employed to serve the artist's own individual sensibility. In the late eighteenth century much of the legacy of Creti's poetic ideals—his landscape settings and idylls—were destined to return as landscape painting and the woodland themes of interior decoration (a specific genre in Bolognese painting).

This process of assimilation begins with the painter Bernardo Mingozzi, who took up the challenge of measuring himself against Creti in Bologna's Palazzo Comunale at the very moment when his predecessor's pictures for Collina Sbaraglia—the paintings forming the basis for the present exhibition—were being installed there.[26]

Notes

1. The background for Creti's formation may be studied in many art-historical writings, i.e. Riccòmini 1965; Roli 1977, *Pittura Bolognese 1650 - 1800*; Bologna 1979, *L'arte del Settecento emiliano. La pittura, l'Accademia Clementina*; Roli 1989, pp. 270-280; Montefusco Bignozzi 1988; Bologna 1990 (essays by Boschloo, Emiliani, Mazza, Riccòmini); Roli 1995. For the scientific and literary context, see: Provenzal 1900; Bologna 1979, *I Materiali dell'Istituto delle Scienze*; Gentili 1989; Raimondi 1987; Cavazza 1990; Bologna 1990 (esp. the essays by Boschloo, Perini, Rave, Riccòmini).

2. Roli 1962, 1967, *Donato Creti*, 1973, *Donato Creti. 46 Disegni inediti* and *Drawings by Donato Creti*; Ruggeri 1974-75.

3. Roli 1967, *Donato Creti*, pp. 14-20; Roli 1990; *Ragguagli sulla prima opera in pubblico di Donato Creti*; Mazza 1992; Mazza, study currently in course of publication.

4. Zanotti 1939, vol. II, pp. 101-102; Roli 1997, pp. 116-117; Mazza 1990, p. I.

5. Volpe in Bologna 1959, p. 162.

6. Zanotti 1739, vol. II, pp. 99-122.

7. Roli 1977, *Pittura Bolognese 1650 - 1800*, pp. 33, 37, 38 and Roli 1989, *La pittura del secondo Seicento in Emilia*, pp. 261-62; Boschloo 1989, pp. 11-21; Perini 1990, pp. XCCVII-CC.

8. Ottani 1966; Bologna 1984. At Palazzo Fava spontaneously sprang up an informal academy of drawing attended by Pasinelli's most promising pupils (cf. Mazza 1990, p. LII).

9. Count Fava's habit of dating each drawing makes it possible to identify with certainty several of them made between 1685 and the end of the century. Cf. Roli 1959, p. 329; 1962, p. 241.

10. Miller 1969, p. 307; 1991, pp. 212-218.

11. Roli 1997, *Pittura Bolognese 1650 - 1800*, p. 116; Miller 1969, p. 307; Mazza 1992, pp. 108, 113.

12. Maylender 1929, vol. I, pp. 26-27; Roli in Pescarmona 1995, p. 22; Riccòmini in Bologna 1990, pp. LXXXII-LXXXIII.

13. Raimondi 1987, ed. 1989, pp. 150-53; Bergamini 1988, pp. 34-37.

14. Zamboni 1979, pp. 211-13; Angeleri 1985; Zamboni 1988, pp. 123-25; Boschloo 1989, pp. 169-171. Beginning in 1712, Creti served nine times as director of the figure-drawing course; he was elected head of the Accademia in 1729. Cf. Farneti 1988, pp. 107-116.

15. Lovarini 1937, pp. 13-15; Zamboni 1979 and 1988; Angeleri 1985 and 1986; Boschloo 1989, pp. 11-43.

16. Roli 1967, *Donato Creti*, pp. 28-29.

17. Mazza 1992, pp. 100-102.

18. Roli 1967, *Donato Creti*, p. 29 and 1977, *Pittura Bolognese 1650 - 1800*, p. 117; Mazza 1990, esp. p. CCXII with a bibliography of earlier publications.

19. Roli 1967, *Donato Creti*, pp. 29-30; Brizzi 1987, p. 113 no. 6; Bernardini 1989, p. 23 no. 9.

20. Roli 1988, *Le scene astronomiche di Donato Creti*, (containing a bibliography of earlier publications); Romano 1978, pp. 106-107; Johns 1992.

21. Zamboni 1979, pp. 213-219; Angeleri 1986, pp. 84-99; Zamboni 1988, pp. 125-129; Boschloo 1989, pp. 27-43.

22. Cf. the summary in Roli 1988, *La pittura del Sei Settecento*, pp. 261-265.

23. Roli 1988, *La pittura del Sei Settecento*, pp. 273-74.

24. Haskell 1963, ed. 1966, pp. 440-442; Roli 1977, *Pittura Bolognese 1650 - 1800*, pp. 22-23.

25. The untranslatable inscription, with overtones of the local dialect, appears in Mazza 1997, p. 114 and runs: "Donato Creti passeggia sulle mura per le sue applicazioni." A rough, if lame, English version might be: "Donato Creti strolls about the walls for his application" [of himself to his task and also, perhaps, of paint to canvas].

26. Grandi 1997, p. 20.

II

Marco Antonio Collina Sbaraglia:
a Pioneer of Modern Cultural Patronage

Fernand de Saint Urbain
Medal of Girolamo Sbaraglia
1709, Museo Civico Archeologico.
Bologna.

Girolamo Sbaraglia memorial
drawing from Donato Creti.
first half of the 18th century.
Christ Church. Oxford.

On June 8, 1710 Girolamo Sbaraglia died in Bologna
at the age of sixty-nine. For around forty years he had
held the chair of medicine and anatomy at the University of Bologna. A competent anatomist and one of a
long line of intellectuals connected with the institution,
Sbaraglia had distinguished himself through his many
publications in the field of medicine.[1] The terms of his
will were destined to have a profound impact on the
city's cultural institutions, since he made his inheritance contingent upon the creation of a public library.
His sole heir was Marco Antonio Collina,[2] who was to
take his benefactor's surname upon accepting the
inheritance. In accordance with Sbaraglia's wishes,
Marco Antonio—who was himself to become famous
for his commitment to cultural institutions and conservation—commissioned the painter Donato Creti and
the sculptor Giuseppe Maria Mazza to create a com-
memorative monument in the inner courtyard of the
Palazzo dell'Archiginnasio, seat of the University.[3] A
drawing (Christ Church College, Oxford) once attributed to Creti, has been thought to derive from Creti's
work;[4] while the surviving original oil sketch[5] is believed to document the beginning of the artist's work
on the project. The oil sketch also marks of Creti's relationship with Collina Sbaraglia, begun a few years earlier, when Creti painted a canvas of *Christ in the House
of Mary and Martha*, later given to the hospital of San
Giovanni in Persiceto.[6]
The effigy of Girolamo Sbaraglia at the center of the
memorial— a work in bronze by Giuseppe Maria Mazza—is derived from the portrait appearing on a medal
by the French medalist Ferdinand de Saint-Urbain,
who had made an important series of such objects in
Bologna for Marcello Malpighi between 1691 and
1693. This fact leads us to suspect that the commem-
oration of Girolamo Sbaraglia was carried out in competition with his more innovative colleague and adver-
sary Malpighi. The same medal that was used as a
model by Mazza was also to form the basis for Sba-

raglia's later iconography and, in particular, for Creti's
etching of him, known in two versions.[8]
Sbaraglia's commitment to the foundation of a public
library reflected a need felt with special urgency in the
climate of cultural renewal of those years, when the
rapid progress of scientific research led to a demand for
new ways of organizing and spreading knowledge: a
function that the Church's extant libraries were ill-
equipped to fulfill.
Conceived in the same as Marsili's plan for the creation
of an Institute of Science, the library project was not to
meet with similar success, despite the large sums of
money and the many books Collina Sbaraglia made
available in support of it.
The Church authorities could not but look unfavorably
on a project which would have undermined the cultural importance of monastic libraries. Furthermore, Collina Sbaraglia found it difficult to maneuver in the
institutional and political situation of Bologna, with its
"mixed government" (explained in greater detail
below), and he was unable to find the right political
backers for a project which would have had a great
impact upon the city's history. His project would have
also solved the problem of another important legacy of
books that had been public property for over a century but had not yet been made accessible to readers: this
was the library left to the Bolognese Senate by the great
naturalist Aldrovandi along with the rest of his vast
scientific collection. Only the part of his inheritance not
composed of books was displayed in the Palazzo Comunale, together with objects donated by the Marchese Ferdinando Cospi in the second half of the seven-
teeth century, whose holdings formed a collection of an
encyclopedic character similar to that of the Wunder-
kammern found throughout central Europe.[9]
The highest political authorities in Bologna were the
Senate and the Papal Legate, the representative of
papal power (the city constituting, at the time, part of
the Papal States). Administrative tasks were divided

29

Hæc est Sbaralæ Medici Doctoris imago,
Ingenio celebris, consilio, arte, libris.
Rapta Anima est Brutis, tribuit quam Numen amicum,
Reddit, hic; hic ergo Numinii instar erit.

Donatus Creti Bononiensis delineavit et sculpsit. 1716.

among various *Assunterie* with responsibility for diverse institutions and services. A project as important as that for a public library could not move foreward without the approval of the Archbishop and Curia, which presided over local church affairs. Collina Sbaraglia encountered more opposition than encouragement. In 1723, even before drawing up plans for a library, he had proposed to the Senate the creation of a Chamber of Geography and Nautical Science and of a related university chair. This project met with official approval in 1744 at great financial cost, and on condition that the chair be entrusted to Collina Sbaraglia's brother, Father Abbondio Collina, a member of the Camaldolite religious order.[10]

In 1730, a first plan was proposed for a public library near the university, in a building formerly occupied by the Ospedale della Vita that was to be bought with funds from the Sbaraglia inheritance. This plan also called for the allotment of public money to pay for the library's continuing growth and efficient administration. The idea, however, aroused suspicion and hostility among the local authorities.

At this point, drawing inspiration from the strategy adopted years earlier by Luigi Ferdinando Marsili in his campaign for the construction of the astronomical observatory in Palazzo Poggi, Collina Sbaraglia tried to deal directly with Rome and to obtain the personal support of Clement XII.

Although his written proposal finally reached the Pope, who declared himself enthusiastic, it came to nought, since every decision was delegated anew to the local authorities, who found new reasons to oppose it.[11]

Bologna was then going through a period of transition marked by the birth of the Institute of Science. From that very institution came a counter-proposal for a public library, one having no connection with the project that was causing Collina Sbaraglia so many difficulties. Although he declared himself quite willing to take part in the new proposal and contribute to its success, he was unable to obtain any important role in its realization.

For various reasons, the plan—the execution of which was entrusted to the Bolognese architect Carlo Francesco Dotti—bore no concrete results until after 1740. Construction of a library in Palazzo Poggi began in 1741, while in 1742, at long last, the Aldrovandi library collections were moved from the Palazzo Comunale to the Institute of Science.[12] Collina Sbaraglia, however, had not yet found a home for his own library, and the project of making the books collected by Girolamo Sbaraglia accessible to the public was not to be solved until 1742.[13] In the meantime, he had done other things for the university: in particular, he had paid for two statues, executed by Ercole Lelli, that had been ordered by the Senate for the anatomy theater, as well as covered the cost for seven other statues commemorating famous physicians, one of which—naturally—represented Girolamo Sbaraglia.[14] These seven statues formed part of a series of sixteen that the Senate was planning to have made for the same anatomy theater.

Collina Sbaraglia thought he spotted a new opportunity to find a home for the vast library he had inherited when the year 1742 saw the beginning of work on a library that was to be open to the public at the Jesuit College at Santa Lucia,[15] another of the city's important cultural centers. He thus found himself turning to an institution where the educational purposes and forms were quite different from those of the schools he had previously approached, for Santa Lucia was the seat of the College of Nobles, open only to future members of the ruling class.[16]

In 1744 Collina Sbaraglia associated himself with the donation to the College of Nobles of the important library of Monsignor Francesco Zambeccari, a dignitary of the Basilica of San Petronio in Bologna. The gift of the two libraries was formalized in a single document, on condition that the library be immediately opened to the public despite the infinite obstacles that had hitherto arisen.[17] So it was that the promoter of the plan for a new public library finally found himself falling back upon the old tradition of a gift to a religious order, albeit the one most advanced in the fields of learning and teaching. Collina Sbaraglia's commitment to his project, however, did not end with his gift to the library of the Jesuits. He intended to donate around 1400 volumes on miscellaneous subjects to an Academy of Erudition and Ancient History that was to be established as part of the Institute of Science. (Although this project also failed, the volumes were later to enter the library of the Institute of Science, joining the Marsili and Aldrovandi collections there at the time when French troops occupied the city.)[18] The year 1744, which brought the resolution to the problem of making Girolamo Sbaraglia's library available to the public, unfortunately also saw the death of his heir Marco Antonio, who was thus deprived of the opportunity of enjoying the satisfactions and honor he had earned through his tireless efforts.[19]

The year he died, he drew up a will leaving to the Senate the paintings he had commissioned from Creti,[20] thus initiating what was to become an ongoing "competition" to donate works of art to the public. This display of civic spirit anticipated the more famous gift by Monsignor Francesco Zambeccari of sixteenth-century religious paintings to the Accademia Clementina in 1762, a donation which was to form the nucleus of the future Pinacoteca Nazionale in Bologna.[21]

The Senate forgot to find a place in the Palazzo Comunale for "memory of gratitude, which [the Senate] ought to have voted to place there as a sign of appreciation,"[22] the splendid portrait of Marco Antonio by Donato Creti, a rare and perhaps unique display of the artist's skill in the genre, eventually went to the Institute of Science.[23]

Marco Antonio Collina Sbaraglia's tale is emblematic of the historical and social situation in Bologna during the early decades of the century, a period characterized by the crisis of the nobility and the rise of newly influential social classes who affirmed their achievements through cultural and artistic activities and patronage.[24] As Renato Roli has observed, Collina Sbaraglia was a figure who, "being unable to shine for nobility of birth or profundity of culture, succeeded in winning a place for himself through intelligent enterprise and generosity." This social context helps explain the institutional-

ized resistance encountered by such innovative programs as those of Sbaraglia and his heir.

The period was crucial for the structuring of the city's cultural and artistic institutions and the formation of its historical and artistic heritage. Under the pontificate of Pope Benedict XIV (1740-1758)—the Bolognese cardinal Prospero Lambertini—the Institute of Science enjoyed a period of particular vitality. During these years, the apartments in the Palazzo Comunale of the Gonfaloniere di Giustizia (the head of the civic administration, elected for a short term) were adorned with works of art, perhaps inspired by Collina Sbaraglia's bequest. To the works that had hung in the apartments since the previous century, other picture were soon added,[25] including one by the celebrated stage designer Ferdinando Bibiena and a series of landscapes specifically commissioned from Bernardo Minozzi, an artist of Bibiena's school whose presence was perhaps particularly gratifying to the elderly Creti, whose collaborator he had been twenty years earlier.[27]

Donato Creti
Experience
about 1713,
oil on copper,
private collection.

Donato Creti
Christ with Martha and Mary
1710, oil on canvas,
San Giovanni in Persiceto,
Bologna.

Donato Creti
Portrait of Marco Antonio
Collina Sbaraglia,
about 1740, oil on copper,
Biblioteca Universitaria,
Bologna.

At the very moment when the Palazzo Comunale renounced any ambitions of becoming a scientific museum or encyclopedic Wunderkammer[28] in favor of the Institute of Science, Collina Sbaraglia endowed it with a nucleus of paintings so important that it could have been opened to the public as a picture gallery.

The passage of French troops through Bologna (1796-1797) and Napoleon's suppression of civic institutions permanently impoverished the Palazzo Comunale's collections. To the Accademia Clementina–which had already been entrusted with the protection and conservation of works of art–went such outstandingly important works as Guido Reni's *Samson* and his famous *Pala della Peste*, along with other works by the school of Raphael and the Carracci. All these pictures were later to enter the present day Pinacoteca Nazionale.

Creti's pictures remained hanging throughout the course of the eighteenth century. They attracted no particular attention during the nineteenth century, when it appears that only some of them were on view. The paintings received scant attention from curators and restorers and by the end of the 1930, any scholar attempting a first reconstruction of Creti's corpus might reasonably have concluded that more than one of the pictures had disappeared. They are not mentioned in the entry by Hermann Voss in *Thieme-Becker*'s dictionary of art—one of the most complete listings of art works available to scholars—while Alcsuti, in his monographic article published in 1932, thought that the two canvases with Mercury and the eight overdoors were lost.[29] Many of the pictures, however, were subsequently displayed in the exhibition of eighteenth-century Emilian art held in the Palazzo Comunale in 1935. The event was the fruit of a large-scale organizational and scholarly effort reflecting the general re-evaluation of Baroque art that was going on in Italy at the time. Promoted by the city government and coordinated by Guido Zucchini, an engineer and technical expert entrusted by the city with matters regarding art display and restoration, the show drew upon contributions from an illustrious group of scholars, including Heinrich Bodmer, Giuseppe Fiocco, Matteo Marangoni, Sergio Ortolani, Hermann Voss and, above all, Roberto Longhi, who had recently been appointed to the chair of art history at the University of Bologna.[30]

On the occasion of the exhibition, Donato Creti's fame improved in two distinct areas. The first regarded the interpretation of his art. In his address inaugurating the 1934 academic year, the great connoisseur and critic Roberto Longhi rhetorically asked: "Who could resist the utter enchantment of those glassy bands of imaginary light, descending upon the distant Two Towers in tones of pale yellow, attenuated green and lapis lazuli in the paintings of your diaphanous, meticulous Donato Creti, the Bolognese Watteau?"[31]

The second area in which Creti's work benefitted from a renewal of interest was conservation and museology. The 1935 exhibition was preceded by an intense restoration campaign that aimed to give back to the Palazzo Comunale its monumental appearance and confer upon it a more important ceremonial role. The creation of a public gallery in the Palazzo was this campaign's logical corollary. The city of Bologna owned many works, mostly paintings and furnishings that had come to it over the years through donations or bequests and had never found a precise permanent location. For example, many works were to be found in the rooms of the police headquarters, formerly the rooms of the Cardinals Legate, whose decorations had been rendered practically invisible both by architectural barriers and by the uses to which they were being put. In the early 1920s, the prevalent view had been the negative, centralized one held by the State-appointed Superintendent of Galleries, Francesco Malaguzzi Valeri, whose policy had been to choose the best works belonging to the city and move them to the Pinacoteca Nazionale. A decade later, however, the situation had evolved in the direction of a renewed civic and municipal awareness.[32] Thus it was that 1936 saw the inauguration, in the presence of the reigning Savoia family, of the Civic Art Collections in the Palazzo Comunale (also known as Palazzo d'Accursio).

The architectural focal point was the Galleria Vidoniana, a Baroque gallery in the Palazzo Comunale that had been created in accordance with the Roman taste of the time on the orders of the Cardinal Legate Pietro Vidoni after the middle of the seventeenth century and now restored to its original spatial scale, with its wall decorations of the Neo-Classical period renewed. No works could have harmonized better than Creti's with the allegorical decorations of the ceiling and the Neo-Classical statues in stucco in fulfilling the desire for a public gallery in the Palazzo Comunale already expressed two centuries earlier in Zanotti's writings. Nor could any other space in the Palazzo have offered a more appropriate setting for these pictures. The whole evokes once more the glories of the times of the Bolognese Pope Benedict XIV Lambertini. The desire to achieve such a re-evocation, implicit in the arrangement of the museum as a whole, reflected a general revival of interest in the eighteenth century that also led to other exhibitions of international importance elsewhere in Italy.

Notes

1. For the career and writings of Girolamo Sbaraglia, the basic text remains Fantuzzi 1789, vol. VII, pp. 332-341. See also Colombo 1987 and Cavazza 1990, pp. 185-201.

2. Roli 1990, *Il Creti a Palazzo*, p. 47 and p. 55, note 4.

3. The medium in which the work was executed, with oil paint being applied directly to the wall, was probably the cause of the rapid deterioration already noted by Creti himself as early as 1717. Cf. Roli 1967, *Donato Creti*, pp. 34-35 and 85-86, no. 5 and sheet no. 30; Riccòmini 1972, p. 109, no. 95; Biagi Maino 1987, pp. 134-37.

4. Lloyd 1969, p. 377 and fig. 56; Ruggeri 1974, p. 23, note 28.

5. Once believed lost, the oil sketch, in very poor condition, is now in the Collezioni Comunali d'Arte di Bologna. Roli 1967, *Donato Creti*, p. 88, no. 33; Grandi 1990, pp. 131-32.

6. Roli 1967, *Donato Creti*, p. 97, no. 95; Roli 1990, *Il Creti a Palazzo*, p. 55.

7. The reverse of the medal shows a leafy tree alluding to the uselessness of Malpighi's painstaking scientific analyses. There are two versions of the medal, one cast and the other stamped; the idealized portrait of Sbaraglia appearing on the latter seems to have been Mazza's primary source, perhaps by way of a drawing after it by Giovan Pietro Zanotti. The medal constitutes the basis of Sbaraglia's subsequent iconography; cf. Noè 1987, pp. 70-71; p. 72, fig. 50; p. 73, fig. 51; p. 77, notes 34-35, 85-86, catalogue entries 20-21.

8. Gaeta Bertelà-Ferrara 1974, nos. 263-263a; Roli 1967, *Donato Creti*, pp. 68 and 100-101; Noè 1987, p. 77, note 37. It was probably derived from a drawing by Creti today at the Archiginnasio's library (Roncuzzi Roversi Monaco, Bologna 1994, p. 122, no. 12).

9. For the Aldrovandi and Cospi collections in the Palazzo Comunale, see Emiliani 1972, p. 43, no. 8; Gentili 1980, pp. 229-233 and Grandi 1985, p. 9.

10. Balsamo 1988, p. 185; Farinelli 1988, p.

74; Roli 1990, *Il Creti a Palazzo*, p. 47.

11. Colombo 1983, pp. 120-125; Colombo 1987, pp. 253-64.

12. For the plans for the library and their history, see Lenzi 1988, pp. 68-78.

13. A homogeneous group of over a hundred volumes (including works by Isaac Newton and other scientists, atlases, and works by Jesuit authors on China and India) had entered the Istituto delle Scienze with the creation of the Camera di Geografia e Nautica; cf. Balsamo 1988, p. 185.

14. Colombo 1982, pp. 11, 129 (note 10), 114; Roli 1990, Il Creti a Palazzo, p. 47.

15. Colombo 1982, p. 127; Balsamo 1988, p. 185.

16. The élite membership of the academies within the colleges was selected on the basis of academic performance. Around 1711-12, Donato Creti painted the canvas showing *Saint Francis Saverio Invoking the Virgin's Protection of Sailors* for the Accademia degli Argonauti; the work is now in the Collezioni Comunali d'Arte di Bologna. Cf. Roli 1967, *Donato Creti*, pp. 86-87, no. 13; Brizzi 1987, p. 115, fig. 6; Brizzi 1988, p. 154.

17. Colombo 1982, pp. 127-128. The collection of books bequeathed by Sbaraglia was highly specialized, dealing primarily with medicine (anatomy, surgery, pharmacology, chemistry), philosophy, natural history, and ethnography, most of which topics were irrelevant to the courses of higher study pursued at the Jesuit institution; cf. Balsamo 1988, p. 188. The collection's subsequent history is bound up with larger events. Some volumes entered the Istituto delle Scienze at the time of the French occupation, while the Biblioteca di Santa Lucia was transferred to the Archiginnasio in 1869 following Italian unification; cf. Balsamo 1988, p. 190. It is important to emphasize the Jesuits' role in providing the citizenry with a library service. The religious order's educational organization ensured continuity and efficiency in this area, continuing to fill a gap in higher learning even after the initiatives undertaken by Marsili; cf. Bal-

samo 1988, pp. 185-86.

18. Balsamo 1988, p. 186.

19. Colombo 1983, p. 128.

20. Roli 1990, *Il Creti a Palazzo*, pp. 47 and 55 and note 1 (containing references to archival documentation).

21. Roli 1990, *Il Creti a Palazzo*, p. 55.

22. Id., ibid.

23. An inscription of later date than the picture itself, identifying the sitter and providing basic biographical information, reads: MARC. ANT. COLLINA SBARAGLI BONON. NAT. 2 FEB. 1681 OB. DIE 28 OCT. 1774. Cf. Roli 1967, *Donato Creti*, p. 86; Benati 1988, pp. 148-49 and p. 143, fig. 6.

24. Benassi 1988, pp. 77-79; Giacomelli 1980.

25. The works include Guido Reni's *Plague Altarpiece* and *Samson*, two sixteenth-century works derived from Raphael, and a large *Saint Caterina de' Vigri* by Marco Antonio Franceschini; cf. Bernardini 1989, p. 11 and Cammarota 1998, pp. 3-7.

26. Roli 1967, *Donato Creti*, p. 56, note 32.

27. Grandi 1997, p. 20; Roli 1967, *Donato Creti*, p. 85, no. 3.

28. In 1742 the Museo Aldrovandiano and the collection of the Marchese Ferdinando Cospi were transferred to Palazzo Poggi; cf. Emiliani 1972, p. 15 and Grandi 1985, pp. 10-11.

29. Roli 1990, *Il Creti a Palazzo*, p. 48 (with a bibliography).

30. Bologna 1935. Among the reviews of the exhibition: Foratti 1935, pp. 21-25; Sandri 1935, pp. 4-10.

31. Longhi's allusion to Watteau, perhaps inspired by Creti's *Idyll* in the Museo di Palazzo Venezia in Rome, is inapplicable to most of Creti's other work; cf. Longhi 1934, ed. 1973, p. 204.

32. Bernardini 1989, pp. 188-93 (with a bibliography).

III

Italy's Most Perfect Paintings

The works that follow—with the lone exception of The *Two Children Playing*—compose a unified group which is of particular interest for at least two reasons. In the first place, they were all painted for a single patron, Marco Antonio Collina Sbaraglia. Furthermore, they constitute the most important group of pictures by Creti to have come down to us intact (another is comprised of the small canvases showing astronomical subjects now in the Vatican Galleries).

Their history is linked to two illustrious figures in the cultural life of the period: Girolamo Sbaraglia, who taught anatomy at the city's famous university, and his heir Marco Antonio Collina Sbaraglia, whose donation of the pictures to the Bolognese Senate created a nucleus of works of art for the collections in the Palazzo Comunale; it was around this nucleus that the Civic Art Collections, founded around 1930, were later to grow.

To the series commissioned by Collina Sbaraglia, another canvas of Creti's also in the City Collections, has been added: the *Two Children Playing*. A free reworking of part of Creti's *memorial to Girolamo Sbaraglia* of 1713, it exemplifies the process of selection and abstraction through which the artist reinterpreted the finest aspects of Bolognese Classicism and Naturalism, especially as expressed by Guido Reni and Simone Cantarini.

The Sbaraglia cycle marks an important moment in Creti's career and is one of the most outstanding examples of art patronage in eighteenth-century Bologna. The most singular aspect of this series of mythological and allegorical paintings, is the way it seems designed along the lines of a frescoed decor. Given the number of pictures and the large size of two of them—*Mercury Giving the Golden Apple to Paris* and *Mercury Bringing the Head of Argus to Juno*, both having practically the dimensions of an altarpiece—we may hypothesize that, from the outset, these works were meant for a public place; for they would constitute a most unusual group indeed in any private residence.

As Giovan Pietro Zanotti, Creti's friend and the historiographer of the Bolognese Accademia Clementina, wrote in 1739, the artist began to work on the series immediately after painting the *memorial* to Girolamo Sbaraglia; these were painted in the Palazzo dell'Archiginnasio, seat of the university. In facts, a list of expenditures, beginning in 1714, records the purchase of large quantities of pigments, above all of impressive amounts of ultramarine blue.[1] Work continued into the third decade of the century: in October 1721, we find payments for priming two "large pictures" (*Mercury and Paris* and *Mercury and Juno*) as well as expenditures for the copper supports for three of the four Virtues (*Humility*, *Prudence* and *Temperance*).[2] It follows that the order in which Zanotti mentions the works (the four Stories of Achilles, the two canvases of Mercury and Paris and Mercury and Juno, the four Virtues, the eight overdoors) does not precisely correspond to their chronology.

It is probable that the moralizing connotations Zanotti found in the *Virtues* also apply to the scenes drawn from Greek and Roman mythology (*Stories of Achilles*, *Mercury and Paris*, *Mercury and Juno*). But Zanotti's literal, rather generic description does not offer much help in the interpretation of the conceptual links among the various works, or their connection with the patron. Nonetheless, his pages constitute our main source of information.

Creti's references to older traditions of symbolism are particularly evident in the *Virtues*, as a perusal of iconographic manuals will reveal. However, Creti overcomes the tendency to abstract conceits and allegorical intellectualization that had prevailed from the late sixteenth century by selecting only elements that had already become so thoroughly conventional as to be utterly and immediately clear in their meaning to his contemporaries. Drawing upon the best precedents that Bolognese culture—and, to a lesser extent, that of the Veneto—had to offer for the rendering of a subject at

Donato Creti
Humility (detail)
about 1719-1721
oil on copper,
Collezioni Comunali d'Arte
di Palazzo d'Accursio,
Bologna.

once naturalistic and classically composed, Creti achieved a narrative and iconographic clarity perfectly in keeping with the reforming tendencies of the beginning of the eighteenth century, above all in the field of literature.

There was surely a more precise intention than we can grasp today underlying the commission for the four accompanying canvases devoted to the myth of Achilles and the two representing *Mercury with Paris* and *Mercury with Juno*. The impression of elusive meanings or intentions is due, in all probability, to the fact that these pictures were not so much components of a literary or philosophical program worthy of being handed down to posterity as one with implied references to a cultural mentality so widespread at the time as to be recoverable only at the level of supposition, by following up clues and hints. The cultural aim was a return to the Greek and Latin classics, viewed as the principal means of simplifying the language of poetry. This was the program promoted by the Bolognese Arcadia in its early years, which advocated a new aesthetic bearing the hallmarks of clarity and rationality.

For many of these pictures there exist, in addition to drawings, oil sketches and autograph replicas and variants. The latter reflect the success of Creti's works with private collectors: above all, with Count Alessandro Fava, the artist's first patron and protector. The production of numerous drawings and oil sketches is part of the painter's particular method of creation, involving the reiteration and "re-presentation" of certain basic ideas, sometimes in several variants but presented in a fresh context that banishes any sense of repetitiveness. This method is derived from the Accademia Clementina's approach to drawing—considered the foundation of artistic creation—and was based upon study from both artistic models (mostly statues, engravings and drawings) and from life (above all nudes, animals and objects). Many of Creti's most felicitous inventions took on an independent life in later replicas or reworkings. In the mid-eighteenth century, a large proportion of these works were to be found in the house of Count Fava, who possessed an enormous number of drawings by the artist, many of single figures or small groups of figures, as we may conclude from an inventory drawn up by Creti himself.

The canvases commissioned by Collina Sbaraglia show

Creti's highly individual approach to painting in different lights and offer an extraordinary opportunity to study his work. For example, there are many passages where "the pictorial weave lets us catch a glimpse of the agile brush as it shuttles back and forth: sometimes in parallel strokes that fill in an area of uniform color; sometimes managed with loving care as it shapes a neck, a wrist, an ankle, or as it hangs and arranges a drapery or adds the highlights to a coiffure or a piece of jewelry; sometimes in quick gestures that establish, with just a few apt strokes, the foreshortening of a puffy sleeve, the narrowing folds of a knotted shawl."[3] This way of painting was rendered possible by that same manual dexterity and facility which had, right from the start of his career, brought the artist international fame as a draftsman. In some cases, the passage of time has made the technical procedures and intermediate stages of painting more visible. The subtle transparency of a drapery or the apparent diaphanousness of a figure is often partly due to drastic overcleanings which have abraded the topmost layers of the pictorial surface, sometimes removing minute finishing touches. These effects can also derive, however, from the gradual absorption of quickly and lightly applied strata of paint (built up in tiny strokes of liquid, nearly weightless color) by the underlying strata, before the paint had dried. The impression of coloristic density, of solidity and overall clarity, is attained above all by the continuous superposition and crossing of the brushstrokes, the fruit of a feverish creative intensity.

It may happen that a figure, already completely built up in its fundamental structural elements, is subsequently covered several times over with repeated layers of drapery, in a practice analogous to that of a sculptor modeling a bozzetto in clay. This practice, surely reinforced by academic study, reaches the point where it is no longer really possible to distinguish between what we would tend, today, to consider a *pentimento* (for example, that baldric covered in unveiled color in the *Mercury and Paris*) and what ought rather to be interpreted as a deliberate, creative procedure (as in the very frequent cases of profiles which are visible one beneath the other, or else are buried in background). The result is that, at one and the same time, profiles have the clarity of a cameo and the delicacy of a veil, and that the pictorial surfaces resemble some highly refined porcelain: in this, as in much else, Creti's position is antithetical to the full-bodied, immediate, "painterly" work being made in Bologna by Giuseppe Maria Crespi during the same years.

Of the series of eighteen pictures painted for Sbaraglia, sixteen are shown here. Two overdoors (*A Woman Sleeping* and *A Seated Woman with a Pheasant*) have not been included; painted in tempera, they have suffered more than the other pictures, especially at the hands of nineteenth-century restorers.

Notes

1. Marcon 1990, pp. 128-129; Roli, *Il Creti a Palazzo*, pp. 51-52.
2. Id., ibid.
3. Roli 1967, *Donato Creti*, p. 39.

Four Episodes from the Life of Achilles

Several stories of Achilles

Giovan Pietro Zanotti, 1739

Creti was over forty when he began work on the episodes from the life of Achilles—probably the first pictures from the cycle commissioned by Collina Sbaraglia.[1] These works are not only among the noblest fruits of the artist's maturity, but also a splendid synthesis of the fundamental components of his style, marking his approximation to aspects of the art of Nicolas Poussin. Like that great representative of the Classical ideal, Creti nourishes his work upon the finest sixteenth-century Venetian painting, turning in the present case to Titian, as well as to Paolo Veronese, whose paintings he had assiduously studied in his youth.

"The lesson of Titian's *Bacchanals*, filtered through the experiences of Annibale Carracci and Albani, found a new Poussin in Creti, but one animated and trembling with varying humors: humors whose agitation manifests itself in the gestures and the way the figures are intertwined, in the infinitely varied way light is reflected, in the edges and vapors torn from the sky by sharply outlined rocky horizons. This is not to say that Creti is led to abandon the inexorable norms of the Bolognese artistic tradition, of which he seems, rather, to be the last, subtle interpreter. There is subtle calculation in his notation of the imagery of this evocative Arcadia, where the staged scenes move to a music moderate in rhythm, naturally imaginative, and at times vaguely languid and passionate with moderation."[2]

Although the passage quoted above refers specifically to the four present pictures, it well expresses the underlying critical context in which we may place Creti's painting as a whole. Interweaving an interpretation of the artist as "eccentric" and "romantic" with a recognition of his more truly academic soul, the passage clarifies the way in which Creti represents a particular sort of Classicism that was to surface anew—obviously in a different form—only at the end of the eighteenth century.

In the course of Creti's artistic development, these pictures stand mid-way between his more loftily academic and theatrically staged works of the immediately preceding years—characterized, above all, by centralized compositions and mirror-image symmetries (as in the *Philip of Macedon* now in the National Gallery, Washington)—and the treatment of landscape as a practically autonomous genre, as found in the Vatican's eight small canvases with astronomical subjects, dating from 1711. In these last-named works, there is already present the spirit of the poetic idyll (a term denoting a type of short poem with a bucolic setting common in the ancient classical world and extremely popular among the poets of the school known as the Bolognese Arcadia). The crucial moment in this evolution of Creti's is represented by the *Pastoral Scene* (Art Gallery, Belfast), one of the most evocative expressions of the idyllic theme, a slightly earlier work than the scenes of Achilles.

Taken as a whole, the works commissioned by Sbaraglia represent a moment of extraordinary concentration on the artistic tradition Creti most loved and on its underlying creative method: the forms and compositional models he was experimenting with can be seen to enrich his formal repertory, which in the following years evolved "by progressive adjustments" towards his finest works.

An element common to all four canvases is the presentation of the protagonists on a sort of rocky stage with a landscape background that is linked to the figural component by means of "wings" formed by woods (*Thetis Plunging Achilles into the Styx*), mountainous (*Chiron Instructing Achilles*), or an open view (as in the urban background in *Achilles Dragging the Body of Hector*).

Cycles of the life of Achilles, whose deeds are recounted by Homer in the *Odyssey* and in the *Iliad* and whose legend was preserved in Roman literature in Statius's *Achilleïs*, are not very common in Italian painting of the late seventeenth and early eighteenth centuries. Creti's cycle focuses less on the moment of the hero's triumph over Hector (shown in the fourth canvas) than on his childhood and education. Emphasis is placed on the relationship between Achilles and Chiron, the most famous of the Centaurs; a figure who, being immortal, recurs in myths set in various epochs. Tradition associates Chiron with education, especially in the field of medicine, since he was the teacher of Aesculapius (in Greek, Asclepios), whom the Greeks and Romans knew as the divine protector of medicine and surgery.[3] Even in Creti's time the name of Chiron brought instruction to mind, even if his predominant association with moral rectitude, prevalent in earlier times and places (including seventeenth-century Bologna), had begun to fade. It is likely that Creti intended an allusion to the merits of his patron or of Collina Sbaraglia's benefactor, as is surely the case with the four figures of *Virtues*; a link with the physician and teacher Girolamo Sbaraglia is almost certain. It may be that Achilles's life, filled with glory despite its brevity, was meant to allude to the initiative and courage Collina Sbaraglia

had himself displayed in his active role in the city's cultural institutions (the University and the Institute of Science, then the two leading seats of scientific and technical learning and instruction). It is even possible that Creti himself suggested a myth that he found congenial, appropriate, and well enough known to be readily understood. One must not forget the intense study the artist had devoted in his youth to the frescoes in Palazzo Fava by the Carracci and their followers; for Creti these works constituted a model for compositional solutions and mythological narration.

We may say that the four scenes of Achilles are representative of an aesthetic trend of their time that involved a rejection of the more arbitrary aspects of Baroque taste. It will be enough to recall the theory on the manner of representing the climatic moment of a story which, in the very year 1713, Antony Ashley Cooper, third Lord Shaftesbury, provided so rich and brilliant a formulation in a famous text addressed to the Roman painter Paolo de Matteis concerning the depiction of the *Choice of Hercules*. Shaftesbury's principal themes include respect for historical accuracy, unity of time and action, simplicity (as opposed to a preference for the capricious and grotesque), and *decorum* (meaning dignity of form and representation). The English theorist called for an appropriate subordination of secondary elements to the principal episode; color should be "reserved," "severe," and "chaste."[4] These dictates are in line with the aesthetic sensibilities the young Creti had absorbed in the artistic and literary climate at Palazzo Fava: a climate forming part of the period's reaction against Baroque taste.

1. Probably it was the frames of these four paintings that were manufactured at the beginning of August, 1714 and subsequently enriched with intaglios between November and December of the same year. They were gilded only after August 6, 1715, as quoted in the already mentioned list of expenditures by Creti for the Baraglia's commission.
2. Roli 1967, *Donato Creti*, p. 36.
3. For Chiron: Graves, 1958, ed. 1967, pp. 375 and 499; Grimal 1951, ed. 1966, pp. 90-91; for Asclepios - Aesculapius: Graves 1958, ed. 1967, pp. 144-146; Grimal 1951, ed. 1996, pp. 53-54.
4. Holt 1957-58, ed. it., Milan 1977, pp. 433-445.

about 1714
Oil on canvas
125x163 cm

Achilles Plunged into the Styx

In this painting, as in the three following it, Creti takes on the task—comparatively new for him—of integrating a narrative subject into a landscape setting. The poetics of the Arcadian literary school provided an important impulse towards the predominance, in the second and third decades of the eighteenth century, of this type of composition over the loftier architectural backgrounds preferred by classicizing taste.

According to the mythological tradition of Greek and Latin poetry the Greek hero Achilles, who was of divine descent by his mother, the marine divinity Thetis, was plunged into the Styx, a river of Hades whose waters had the power to confer invulnerability. Rather than a sinister, infernal scene appropriate to Hades, the setting here recalls another Styx that flowed through Arcadia. In the lower left is the river god; the winged child flying above the group of females represents—here as in the following two scenes—the Genius (tutelary spirit) of Achilles, as we learn from Creti's associate and biographer Zanotti. These two figures bind in a sort of chiasm the two splendid female servants who, at the center of the scene, hold the infant Achilles. According to Zanotti, the

nymph Thetis is portrayed as an onlooker for reasons of "decorum" and "dignity;" the group of watching girls surrounding her underscores the central episode and creates a practically contrapuntal sequence of faces, gestures, poses, and colors. The lighting is unnatural and restless as it plays over the figures; the servant with her arm around Thetis is like an apparition emerging from the shadows in the light of a candle, despite the glancing highlight on her shoulder; this passage might have been imagined by Parmigianino. Both the principal figures and those off to the sides are seen in a refined, artificial stage-lighting against a landscape where the tonalities are equally unreal, ranging from nocturnal effects to the light of dawn, in a virtuoso display of color. Color is, in fact, the real subject of this canvas. Starting from a few basic hues—ultramarine, white, yellow, brown—Creti progressively builds up tints, and intermediate tones through superimposed layers and glazes. An external confirmation of the extent to which this painting represents a culminating point in Creti's exploration of the idyllic theme comes from a comparison with a drawing of *Venus and Adonis* (or *Diana and Endymion*) now in the Pinacoteca Na-

zionale in Bologna, where there appears in the background the same detail of embracing, practically dancing nymphs.[1]

A preparatory canvas offering several variants is in a private collection in Bologna (Benati 1995; temporarily exhibited with the Civic Art Collections, *Incontri & Arrivi* 2, November 1996— January 1997). For other versions or replicas, see Roli 1967, p. 92 and Roli 1990, pp. 48-49, fig. 2. A few years earlier, the artist had dealt with the theme in an oval canvas of unfinished appearance, painted mostly in tones of blue-gray; the work is now in the Pinacoteca Nazionale, Bologna (Roli 1967, *Donato Creti*, pp. 36-88). A preliminary drawing for this last work is in the Metropolitan Museum of Art in New York (Roli 1973, p. 28 and Bean 1979, p. 121, no. 152).

Notes
1. Roli, 1967, *Donato Creti*, p. 105, no. 10.

Bibliography
Zanotti 1739, II, pp. 111-112; Oretti B. 130, c. 162; Zaist 1774, II, p. 127; Bassani 1917, p. 20; Alcsuti 1932, p. 45; Zucchini 1934, p. 57, 60; Bologna 1935, p. 31, no. 1; Zucchini 1938, p. 66; Roli 1959, p. 334; Roli 1967, Donato Creti, p. 87; Roli in Bologna 1977, p. 29, 117.

about 1714
Oil on canvas
125x163 cm

Achilles Entrusted to Chiron

Color rather than drawing is the protagonist of the composition, serving to model and describe the flesh areas, to modulate the depths and the folds of the draperies, and to construct a setting independent of any perspective framework. The rich and balanced range of chromatic gradations is built up on the basis of a few basic colors—blue, white, yellow, brown—carefully measured in their application and brushwork (sometimes broad and liquid, sometimes more dense and fine), so as to unite figures and landscape. Each figure is finished according to its importance and function in the scene, and so as not to disturb the relationship between figures and landscape. It is partly on account of a softer definition of outlines and relief that the two women holding urns at the left appear to be placed behind the plane where the principal event is occurring. The same may be said of the mountains and of the enchained figure on the rocky crag. These figures are, so to speak, only roughed in, so that they recede into the background and amalgamate themselves with it in accordance with a method worked out and applied more thoroughly in the fourth canvas of the series. By contrast, the figure of Achille's Genius, meticulously finished and powerfully three-dimensional, has slightly

softened contours that serve to immerse it more thoroughly in the surrounding atmosphere: an effect even more marked in the preceding picture. This intellectual calibration of the whole does not, however, entail a rejection of the artist's fundamentally naturalistic training. Thetis's handmaidens, with their admirable contrapposto, give the infant Achilles to the centaur Chiron "so that he may raise him, instructing him in those things needful to a hero," as Zanotti tells us; while the Genius, from "up in the air, urges him on and accompanies him. Most admirable of all is a young woman in the foreground, half nude and with her back to the viewer, so well executed, and so graceful in symmetry, and of so lovely a color, that one could not wish for more." One of Creti's most felicitous inspirations, this is a nude able to withstand comparison with the finest achievements of European painting of a century later.
Chiron lived on Mount Pelion in Thessaly. There, according to one of the many myths comprising the cycle of the Argonauts, Achilles's father Peleus had been enchained to a rocky crag prior to his marriage to Thetis. Creti must have been well acquainted with this episode, since it occurs in the famous Palazzo Fava fresco cycle of which he had made a thorough study

in his youth. It would therefore appear that Zanotti is wrong when he tells us that the enchained figure represents "the divinity who regulates the waters flowing down a cliff;" for the same reason, the identification of the figure as Prometheus—perhaps the first identification that occurs to the spectator—might be equally erroneous.
It was also on Mount Pelion that the wedding of Thetis and Peleus was celebrated, and it was on that occasion that the goddess Discord placed on the banquet table the apple later given to Paris, so that he could, in turn, assign it to the goddess he judged most beautiful: Venus, Minerva, or Juno. The central group of figures with Thetis and her servant returns in the admirable canvas representing *Artemisia Drinking Mausolus's Ashes* in the collection of Sir Denis Mahon in London, perhaps the same work cited as having once been in Palazzo Fava (Finaldi in Bologna 1998, p. 56, n. 8).

Bibliography
Zanotti 1739, II, pp. 111-112; Oretti B. 130, c. 162; Zaist 1774, II, p. 127; Bassani 1917, p. 20; Alcsuti 1932, p. 45; Bologna 1935, p. 31, n. 1; Zucchini 1938, pp. 61, 66, 68; Roli 1959, p. 334; Paris 1960, nos. 212; Roli 1967, *Donato Creti*, p. 87; Roli 1977, *Pittura Bolognese 1650 - 1800*, p. 29, 117; Roli 1990, *Il Creti a Palazzo*, pp. 48-49.

about 1714
Oil on canvas
125x163 cm

Achilles Instructed by Chiron

This is perhaps the picture that best exhibits Creti's attachment to the most poetic and naturalistic vein of the Carraccis' early painting, sixteenth-century Venetian tradition, and the coloristic refinement of Reni. The composition contains fewer figures and thus highlights the artist's method of building up the whole, a method that will become even more apparent in the overdoors. Creti lays in areas of color over the preparation by using a soft, broad brushstroke. Other, equally layers, are progressively brushed in until zones representing mountains, sky, water, or the rocky "stage" where the action will be set are established. Further layers confer depth on the sky, establish the rocky "wings" of the "stage set," model the volumes, define the areas of light and shade, and slowly, stubbornly heighten the relief. What becomes clear is the central role color plays in Creti's work: not so much as physical substance or as over-all hue or tonality, or even as a means of communicating immediacy of expression, but rather as a product of manual skill, comparable

to what a sculptor does when he works in stucco or clay. Creti's final steps are to reinforce the outlines, sometimes (as in Achilles's sleeve) with a line as light as it is incisive; to emphasize details, occasionally (as in the delicate stream of blood issuing from the slain lion) using extremely diluted colors; and to correct his coloring with transparent glazes. With time the coloristic harmonies have inevitably altered; in certain cases the contrasts are exaggerated than they once were.

The effects of lightness and delicacy in the handling of the draperies reach peaks of virtuosity in Achilles's sleeve, in the lilac-colored edge of the cloak, in the ribbon that appears to attach the quiver to the Genius's wings.

The putti's immersion in the atmosphere of the sky has been obtained by darking them with the same blue used for the underlying stratum. Even when shapes have been little more than sketched in, their volume is well delineated.

The delicate tonalities and diaphanous transparency of these pictures recall Guido

Reni's late works, even that *non finito* [unfinished] quality so typical of his work of that period. There is, in addition, an intellectual, subtly melancholy vein, deriving from the evocative and naturalistic early work of the Carraccis—the young Annibale in particular—in Palazzo Fava. Here is Zanotti's description of the scene of Chiron teaching Achilles the use of the bow and arrow: "The bow sends the arrows where [Achilles] wishes, and on the ground there is a lion he has already shot. In an admirable invention [Chiron] turns to give him another bow so that he may be ready to shoot other beasts." The scene is admired from above by Thetis "courted by various Genii."

Bibliography
Zanotti 1739, II, pp. 111-112; Malvasia-Zanotti 1755, p. 180; Oretti B. 130, c. 162; Zaist 1774, II, p. 127; Alcsuti 1932, p. 45; Zucchini 1938, pp. 61, 66, 68; Roli 1959, p. 334; Bassani 1817, p. 20; Paris 1960, no. 213; Roli 1967, *Donato Creti*, p. 87; Roli 1967, *Peintures de Donato Creti*, p. 251-254; Roli 1977, *Pittura Bolognese 1650 - 1800*, pp. 29, 117; Roli 1990, *Il Creti a Palazzo*, pp. 49-50.

about 1714
Oil on canvas
125x163 cm

Achilles Dragging the Corpse of Hector

Tied to the triumphal chariot, Hector's corpse is dragged over the battlefield and, as Zanotti says, "everywhere is spread a certain horror that both disturbs and delights." The episode is recounted in Book XXIV of the *Iliad*. Above, Thetis goes up Mount Olympus to intercede with Jupiter (*Iliad*, XXIV, 14-21). The walls of Troy have been transformed into a sort of parapet, beyond which unfolds a view of Rome. The painting reveals a reference to models and a complex transmutation of forms typical of Creti's work. The sensation of the familiar—of déjà vu—nonetheless has more to do with a broad visual heritage than with direct quotations: Creti's practice of reformulation results in an evocative and original recreation of forms. In the bodies scattered on the ground at the right, the source of inspiration is probably Guido Reni's (1575 - 1642) *Samson*; but concealed by a series of meditations. The same is true of those passages where the reference to Roman reliefs is readily apparent.

As in other works by Creti, what at first seems a rational composition constructed along lines running either oblique to the picture plane or parallel with it, camouflages irrational pictorial solutions: an intersection and superposition of viewpoints and areas of light and shade, of perfectly finished figures and others that fade into the penumbra, with the unexpected appearance of supernumeraries who surely have something to do with the theatrical practice of the day. The principal viewpoint seems to be from high on the left: it is from here that we observe both the group of Achilles and Hector and the battlefield itself. But other passages—the two men in armor at the sides, the horses and the chariot wheel—presuppose a practically direct frontal view. This is a composition in which even the perfect, almost obsessive decorative details of the chariot, of Achilles's greaves, and of the armor, are at one with the pervasive elegiac mood that encompasses everything from the fantastic sunset, with the backlit Roman cityscape in the distance, to the carefully arranged group of objects in the foreground. The latter constitutes a sort of refined *vanitas*: striking an abstract note seemingly unparalleled in the still-life painting of the time, this passage seemingly reflects the taste for heraldic groupings typical of the Bolognese tradition of illusionistic *quadratura* painting. "In this carefully controlled demonstration of graphic and compositional skill emerges a presentiment of a nearly Romantic melancholy: perhaps the David who painted the *Death of Bara* (Musée Calvet, Avignon) would not have disdained the youthful body of Hector." (Riccòmini 1974, p. 27, no. 13).

Bibliography
Zanotti 1739, II, pp. 111-112; Oretti B. 130, c. 162; Zaist 1774, II, p. 127; Bassani 1817, p. 20; Alesuti 1932, p. 45; Zucchini 1938, p. 68; Roli 1959, p. 334; Roli 1967, *Donato Creti*, p. 87; Riccòmini 1974, p. 27, no. 13; Roli 1977, *Pittura Bolognese 1650 - 1800*, pp. 29, 117, 253; Roli in Bologna 1979, pp. 60-61, no. 103; Roli 1990, *Il Creti a Palazzo*, pp. 48-50.

The Virtues

Four additional pictures on four large copper roundels

Giovan Pietro Zanotti, 1739

The four *tondi* representing *Virtues* well exemplify one of the most incisive critical definitions of Creti's work: "An inherited figurative tradition... the core of which, enriched and fleshed out over the course of two centuries, is still that of the Italian Renaissance;" in turn, Creti bequeathed this heritage "to the Neo-Classicism which was just around the corner and to the next century."[1]

In these works Creti's process of selection among inherited forms reached such an advanced state as to render his sources of inspiration nearly unrecognizable. At times he achieves a classical effect utterly unnatural in its intensity—a kind of lucid abstraction. His works embody an obsession for beauty of form redolent of Raphael, even though Zanotti tells us of Creti's distaste for that painter's work and for all its seventeenth-century Classical derivations, including the paintings of Domenichino and Francesco Albani.[2] The Neo-Renaissance appearance of these *Virtues*—especially of the three set against architectural backgrounds—can be accounted for both within a Bolognese and a North Italian context. The direct source of inspiration is Simone Cantarini, whose Neo-Raphaelesque style, with its gleaming, Venetian-inspired colors possesses a classical monumentality, as seen in the artist's *Rest on the Flight into Egypt* (Brera, Milan).[3] This courtly classicism, reminiscent of works of the later Italian Renaissance, is linked to Venetian traditions, first assimilated by the young Creti in the workshop of Lorenzo Pasinelli and culminating in a trip to Venice which, according to recent research, the artist made in the company of Pietro Ercole Fava. Some of the drawings Creti made after paintings by Paolo Veronese survive.[4] The first work he exhibited in public after his return to Bologna, a *Saint Gregory Giving Alms* now known only from an oil sketch and the preparatory drawing,[5] already concentrated upon the integration of figures into a nobly monumental architectural setting of a clearly classical type.

In the great Renaissance painters of the Veneto, Creti sought naturalness and attention to color, almost as though attempting to recapitulate the "curriculum" of the youthful painters of the Carracci family a century earlier.

Creti's adversion to Raphael—a model seemingly indispensable to any work in a classicizing style—may be explained by reference to Bolognese culture. The year 1678—when Creti was on the point of beginning his precocious artistic career—saw the publication in Bologna of Carlo Cesare Malvasia's *Felsina pittrice*. This text—of fundamental importance for the Bolognese school—adopts a strongly polemical tone towards Raphael, and Tuscan and Roman art in general.[6] For Malvasia an interest in antiquity acquired archaeologizing implications, subsequently echoed by Luigi Ferdinando Marsili, founder of the Academy of Science and a moving spirit behind the Accademia Clementina. Antiquity came to represent a source for nourishing creativity by drawing upon a repertory of formal solutions.

In Bologna, however, the desire for a deeper knowledge and interpretation of ancient Classical culture, with its aesthetic canons and creative roots, never developed into the sort of overriding force that it became in Rome and Florence. Creti's references to antiquity form part of an ongoing search for an absolute ideal of beauty, as is apparent in the figure of *Temperance*.

If the expenditures recorded by the artist in December of 1715 for "four iron hoops to place behind the frames, and round frames for the pieces of copper" already refer to these *tondi*, then the conception and execution of the four pictures may have been a prolonged process continuing over several years. Only in October of 1721 is there a mention of payment "for the three pieces of copper, for painting upon them representations of *Humility, Prudence*, and *Temperance*."[7] Since the document does not mention *Charity*, we may take it that this fourth picture has a separate history.

The *Virtues* reveal Creti's extraordinary skill in uniting symbolism with beauty and naturalism. In this regard, as in others, Venetian High Renaissance art had much to teach him. Steeped in a culture of symbol and allegory, it nonetheless melded such components with a profound feeling for Nature, being, in this regard, unlike Tuscan and Roman art, where these elements were modified by being viewed through the more intellectual and elaborate lens of style.

With this splendid creative moment marked by the *Virtues* can be linked numerous analogous female figures, either Biblical or allegorical. Among them are the allegorical drawings representing *Meditation*,[8] *Study*,[9] and *Painting*.[10]

1. Riccòmini, 1974 p. 17; Roli 1967, *Donato Creti*, p. 38.
2. Roli 1967, *Donato Creti*, p. 76 and Roli in Pescarmona 1995, p. 170.
3. A.M. Ambrosini Massari in Emiliani 1998, p. 160; Mazza, ibid. p. 378.
4. Mazza, 1992, pp. 111-113 and in Emiliani 1998, p. 378.
5. Roli 1990, *Ragguagli sulla prima opera in pubblico di Donato Creti*, pp. 129-135; Mazza 1992, pp. 113-114; Roli in Pescarmona 1995, p. 166 no. 52.
6. Malvasia 1678.
7. Marcon 1990, p. 128.
8. Bologna, Pinacoteca Nazionale, inv. 1845 (Giannattasio in Faietti-Zacchi 1998, p. 266, no. 88).
9. Giannattasio in Faietti Zacchi 1998, p. 266.
10. Paris, Ecole des Beaux Arts; Caracciolo 1993, fig. 15.

about 1719–1721
Oil on copper
diam. 79 cm

Prudence

"She holds a death's head in one hand, and a book in the other, and facing her is a young boy holding up a mirror, as if to say that seeing oneself clearly is no mean part of prudence, as is the thought of our ending, and this is the true science to be learned" (Zanotti). Creti's allegory of *Prudence* maintains the fundamental attributes of the elaborate Mannerist and seventeenth-century treatments of the subject (often represented with two palandromic faces; cf. Ripa 1603, p. 416), formulating its conceits in an incisively schematic, didactically effective fashion. Traditionally, Prudence wears a golden helmet encircled by a mulberry wreath, as an admonition that "the wise and prudent man does not do things before the time is right," but instead arranges them "in an orderly fashion and with decorum" (Ripa 1603, pp. 417-18). Here the helmet lying on the ground becomes the pretext for an outstandingly brilliant passage of painting, counterpointed by the objects forming a discreet vanitas in the background: the books on the ground and the pearl around the vase emitting smoke—allusions to the transience of wordly goods. The skull in no

way disrupts the quality of elegance underscored by the crystalline profile and the position of the arms, with one drawn back, flexed into a right angle and resting upon the high plinth, and the other extended forward, as in the noblest examples of classical sculpture.

The effect owes much to the harmonious juxtaposition of the white of the robe with the blue of the draperies; draperies have such an important role in Creti's pictures as to almost take on a life of their own, as in the *Charity* and the *Humility*. *Prudence*, *Temperance* and *Humility* show a marked tendency towards abstraction that sets them apart from *Charity*.

A female figure having a connection with this Virtue appears in the center of a small oval canvas of *The Glorification of Saint Anthony of Padua* now in the Louvre, ordered by Count Alessandro Fava as a pendant to a similar oil sketch for a never-executed work (Kaufmann Schlagete 1987, p. 121, no. 48: Rosenberg 1984, p. 94, no. 31; Zanotti 1939, vol. II, p. 311).

This particularly inventive moment in the artist's career also produced a drawing now

in the Pinacoteca Nazionale, Bologna, a female figure seated upon a throne with a tall base (inv. 315/1900 cf. Roli 1967, p. 37 and fig. 118; Gaeta Bertelà 1977, p. 34, no. 65), that shows close analogies with the painting of the *Libyan Sybil* (Boston, Museum of Fine Arts; Roli 21988, *Una insolita Veronica di Donato Creti*, p. 326, fig. 2). Partial preparatory studies for the *Prudence* include a study of a male arm appearing on the verso of a drawing in the Pinacoteca Nazionale. Bologna showing *Endymion Asleep* and dated 1719 (inv. 261/1846; Roli 1967, p. 105, no. 7). Attention has been drawn to a figure related to this *Prudence* appearing on a page of sketches in the Lugt Collection (Paris-Florence 1988, cat. pp. 27-28, no. 55: not reproduced here).

Bibliography
Zanotti 1739, II, p. 113; Zaist 1774, II, p. 127; Bassani 1817, p. 20; Voss 1913, p. 101; Alesuti 1932, p. 10, 12; Zucchini 1934, p. 57; Bologna 1935, p. 32, no. 8; Zucchini 1938, p. 70, no. 19; Roli 1959, p. 335; Roli 1967, *Donato Creti*, p. 88; Roli in Bologna 1979, p. 61-62, no. 105.

about 1719–1721
Oil on copper
diam. 79 cm

Temperance

As with *Charity*, the composition of *Temperance* is evocative of the Renaissance. However, the conventional symbolic apparatus indicated by Cesare Ripa (1603, pp. 480-82) has been reduced: a harness, symbolizing the obligation to "check and moderate the appetites of the soul," and the palm branch, "which raises itself back, unbent," indicating victory over the passions. The boy pouring water from one urn into another is an allusion to a traditional attribute not shown here: hot iron tempered with water.

The colors are more attenuated than in *Charity*. There are passages where the draperies have been shaded with transparent lakes applied as glazes or blended with the colors, as in the green on the left side of the figure and the lilac areas of the boy's draperies, which stand out against a pink-streaked sky that is the result of a profound study of the art of Paolo Veronese (1528-1588). There is a pentimento in the red mantle. The plinth upon which the

Virtue sits is articulated by steps running parallel to the picture plain; this motif recurs in many of Creti's allegorical and Biblical figures of this period, including *Prudence*. In both works, the artist's interest went beyond a naturalistic coherence among the parts; the same may be said of the canvas representing *Achilles Dragging the Body of Hector*.

A comparison may be drawn between the *Temperance* (and the *Prudence*) and the beautiful *Sybil* in the Museum of Fine Arts in Boston (Murphy 1985, p. 68; Roli 1988, *Una insolita Veronica di Donato Creti*, p. 326, fig. 2).

Bibliography
Zanotti 1939, II, p. 113; Zaist 1774, II, p. 127; Bassani 1817, p. 20; Voss 1913, p. 101; Alcsuti 1932, p. 10, 12; Zucchini 1934, p. 57; Zucchini 1938, p. 70, no. 20; Bologna 1935, p. 32, no. 8; Roli 1959, p. 335; Roli 1967, p. 88; Roli 1977, *Pittura Bolognese 1650 - 1800*, p. 117, 253; Roli in Bologna 1979, p. 61-62, no. 105.

about 1719–1721
Oil on copper
diam. 79 cm

Charity

In *Charity*, Creti treats allegory in a more markedly naturalistic fashion. According to Zanotti, the work portrays Creti's wife Francesca Zani along with the couple's three young sons (Francesca was the niece of a Bolognese man of letters, and died in 1719). It is not known when Creti began work on this picture, and the date is perhaps not indicative of the real chronology (Roli 1990, pp. 51-52). What is certain is that Creti had previously recorded the features of his pretty young spouse in drawings. At any rate, stylistic analysis tends to support the thesis that this painting was begun independently of other three *tondi*, which are recorded in Creti's list of expenditures from 1721 onwards.

The composition differs from those of the other three, which are more vertical and classical in their architectural backgrounds. The gold-green curtain links the picture with its frame and creates an inward-moving circular rhythm culminating in the central group of the woman and child, depicted with luminous flesh tones against a white couch. As Roli has observed, this solution is rooted in an older visual culture, assimilated and elaborated upon through an infinite number of filters, first and foremost through the simpler inventions of Simone Cantarini. The *Charity* belongs to that line of exploration which was to lead the artist to the felicitous invention of the overdoor with the *Sleeping*

Woman with an Amorino, and which produced a great number of sketches and drawings showing prone figures asleep or startled from sleep with accompanying figures who impart movement to the various hangings (as does the putto holding up the curtain in the present painting). Examples of the genre, which can be traced to the late work of Guercino, had been produced in the shop of Lorenzo Pasinelli and Giovan Gioseffo dal Sole.

But in this case, too, Creti's explorations seem to lead back directly to Venetian models: perhaps to Titian's depictions of *Danaë* and the works deriving from it, which the artist would certainly have seen during his sojourn in Venice. The effects of the fabrics, with the yellow, green, and golden tones that modulate the drapery of the curtain, and the various gradations of blue and azure, are surely the fruit of a subtle distillation of Venetian colorism in conjunction with the refined hues of Guido Reni. The broad red drapery, where the play of the folds appears to function independently of the composition, seems particularly abstract. Thanks to the copper support and the dense application of paint, the colors have not altered—as they have in Creti's canvases—and the balance of color in the composition remains perfect, even among such difficult-to-harmonize hues as red, blue, white, and green.

Among the studies of prone figures related

to the present composition, with its curtain motif and the secondary figure holding up the curtain, a particularly noteworthy comparison is with a drawing of a *Sleeping Cupid* inscribed in an oval which was sold at auction in the early 1970s (cf. *The Burlington Magazine*, no. 851, April 1973, p. XIX). There are analogies in the treatment of the curtain and in the Cantarini-like naturalism the figure shares with the sleeping infant in our painting.

This last-named, pleasing detail, with its extraordinary naturalism, turns up in numerous subsequent works. It is found in a canvas in a private collection in Bologna (Roli 1967, p. 38; Roli 1990, p. 50) and is copied in a painting once in the Louvre but lost during the nineteenth century and now known to us through engravings (Roli 1967, p. 92, no. 54). A drawing formerly attributed to Cantarini is now in the Fondazione Cini, Venice (Roli 1967, p. 38), while another one has appeared on the art market (London, Christie's, July 2, 1991).

Bibliography
Zanotti II, p. 113; Zaist 1774, II, p. 127; Bassani 1817, p. 20; Voss 1913, p. 101; Alesuti 1932, p. 10,12; Zucchini 1934, p. 57; Zucchini 1938, p. 70, no. 20; Bologna 1935, p. 31, no. 5; Roli 1959, p. 335; Roli 1967, *Donato Creti*, p. 88, no. 29; Roli in Bologna 1979, p. 61-62, no. 105; Roli 1990, *Il Creti a Palazzo*, pp. 50-52.

about 1719–1721
Oil on copper
diam. 79 cm

Humility

"Simply but elegantly dressed, she is seen in the act of stooping and bending, thus teaching that the humble man must yield to the wise wishes of the others;" the nearby lamb "signifies that Humility brings with it gentleness" (Zanotti). A fine, recently published sketch, with some slight variations (Biagi Maino, awaiting publication), clarifies the felicitous link between Creti's art and the naturalistic classicism of Simone Cantarini and the final, stylized result. Worked out in a very refined color scale of grays and blues, the *Humility* opens the way for that pursuit of absolute purity of form in the figure, which is here seen against a geometric setting with no naturalistic elements. The same phenomenon characterizes several of the overdoors. The fleeting shadows do not weaken the sculptural firmness of the composition, which nevertheless can accommodate passages of extremely delicate brushwork; an example is the gilded effect produced by the subtle threads of color illuminating the putto's wings and outlining his draperies.

A study connected with the lower part of the figure is now in the Biblioteca Ambrosiana, Milan; as Ruggeri points out, the drawing has close morphological analogies with many of Creti's paintings, such as the figure of *Experience* in the *Sbaraglia memorial* (Ruggeri 1974-75, p. 22 and p. 34, fig. 17). The drawing gives that same impression of the draperies' having a life of their own that we have noted in the *Virtues* and brings to mind Marco Benefial's objection, upon seeing two important works by Creti that had just arrived in Rome (*Jacob's Dream* and *Jacob Struggling with the Angel*), that such "folds and the way of handling them" made the draperies look "not like cloth, but like paper or coral" (Roli 1967, p. 40; Ruggeri 1974-75, p. 22). This judgment betrays Benefial's failure to grasp the modernity implied by the rise of classicism over naturalism that had already entered the tradition of his day.

Bibliography
Zanotti 1939, II, p. 113; Zaist 1774, II, p. 127; Bassani 1817, p. 20; Voss 1913, p. 101; Alesuti 1932, p. 10, 12; Zucchini 1934, p. 57; Zucchini 1938, p. 70, n. 19; Bologna 1935, p 32, no. 9; Roli 1959, p. 335; Roli 1967, *Donato Creti*, p. 88; Roli 1977, *Pittura Bolognese 1650 - 1800*, p. 117, 253; Roli in Bologna 1979, p. 61-62, no. 107; Roli 1990, *Il Creti a Palazzo*, p. 32, no. 9.

The Overdoors

Eight pictures to be placed over doors, painted in monochrome

Giovan Pietro Zanotti, 1739

The eight overdoors represent four male and four female figures. Their original arrangement is unknown, as is the number of rooms in which they were distributed; nonetheless, compositional and technical considerations make it possible to suggest certain groupings. Unlike the other six pictures, all executed in oil, the *Seated Woman with a Pheasant* and the *Sleeping Woman*—neither included here—are in tempera, and constitute a self-contained pair. To judge by their shared technical and stylistic characteristics, the *Nude with a Putto* and the *Sleeping Youth with Winged Putto* almost certainly form a matched pair as well. It is harder to establish a sequence for the remaining four pictures, all more carefully finished and of higher quality. Among them, the *Girl Meditating* stands out for the markedly sculptural rendering that makes it resemble a stucco high-relief and for its generally light tonalities (characteristics recurring, to a certain extent, in the *River God* and the *Enchained Male Nude*). The Girl Holding a Flower may be linked with the Enchained Male Nude and the *Girl Meditating*, as suggested by similarity in the dimensions of the figures and the similar viewpoints adopted.

Even if every attempt at a detailed accounting of the overall iconography seems destined to fail,[1] it is nonetheless possible to recognize some common denominators: a derivation from mythological themes and the representation of various psychological states associated with the theme of tranquillity (meditation, a state of dreaminess, utter relaxation, sleep). To seek an allusion to the artist's own existential condition in these pictures would mean imposing an overly romantic interpretation. At the same time, it is difficult to avoid sensing the presence, in the group as a whole, of a deeply-felt melancholy and dark vein that insinuates itself even where the ostentatious display of academic training in study from the posed model would appear to prevail. While the choice of figures is surely connected to some extent with the rooms where the pictures were meant to be seen, the lack of documentary evidence regarding the furnishing in Collina Sbaraglia's residence prevents us from drawing any firmer conclusions.

On account of the condition in which they have come down to us, the two overdoors omitted from this exhibition (*Sleeping Woman* and *Seated Woman with a Pheasant*) cannot withstand comparison with the other six. The use of tempera has had a negative effect on their conservation, Creti's authorship of the *Sleeping Woman* is demonstrated by two drawings: one formerly in the Krautheimer Collection, New York cited by Roli, in which the woman appears as *Venus Unveiled by an Amorino*,[2] and the one in the Schloss Fachsenfeld Collection, Stuttgart, first published by Christel Thiem and republished by Roli.[3]

The *Seated Woman with a Pheasant* fits naturally into the period when Creti was exploring the idyllic theme: a phase marked by a ceaseless production of drawings, only some directly connected with paintings. There are, for example, a number of sheets showing single figures in mythological or vaguely pastoral landscapes. (Creti, with his aristocratic taste, did not much favor the bucolic genre.) Some of these drawings are now in the Uffizi, Florence, the Pinacoteca Nazionale, Bologna and one is in The Metropolitan Museum, New York.[4] As for the Pinacoteca's drawing of a *Woman Asleep in a Wood*, there exists a variant of the figure of the woman sleeping in a semi-reclining pose where the figure's sinuous contours clarify Creti's relationship to Mannerist painting. More particularly, it leads us back to the *Saint Margaret* in Parmigianino's Santa Margherita Altarpiece, painted in 1527 for the church of the same name and now in the Pinacoteca in Bologna.[5]

So far as the condition of these works is concerned, the majority have suffered losses. Many subtle finishing touches, executed with fine brushstrokes, have vanished: these include details of hair and ornaments, as well as certain passages in the landscapes and draperies.[6]

1. R Roli 1990, *Il Creti a Palazzo*, p. 50.
2. Roli 1990, ibidem, and p. 54, fig. 7.
3. Thiem 1983, pp. 122-23, no. 65; Roli 1990, ibidem, pp. 50 and 53, fig. 6.
4. Roli 1967, *Donato Creti*, p. 37-38.
5. P. Giannattasio in Faietti-Zacchi, 1998, pp. 270-271, no. 90.
6. Further evidence is provided by certain old photographs now in the collection of the Kunsthistorisches Institut, Florence.

about 1715–1721
Oil on canvas
105x175 cm

A Girl Holding a Flower

This work, perhaps representing *Spring*, and the *Girl Meditating* were selected for the 1979 Biennale bolognese d'arte antica, because they represent the two expressive registers that always coexist in Creti's painting: a "proto-Neoclassical" vein, on the one hand, and, on the other, a more "sentimental" and Romantic one (Roli 1979, p. 62). Both traits presage the sweetness and elegiac beauty that were later to characterize certain small, independent paintings, such as the allegorical figures in the museum at Tours (Roli 1967, *Peinture de Donato Creti*, p. 255).

In *Girl Holding a Flower*, Creti achieves an emotional fusion of figure with landscape that represents a virtuoso high point of chiaroscuro monochrome technique, with effects varying from vibrant gradations of atmospheric density and depth to the simulation of a range of colors. The woman's body is classically rounded, the draperies sometimes brittle and firm, sometimes light and fluid; the penumbra shadow playing on her face poetically harmonizes these diverse elements.

The image is built up from extremely thin layers of pigment, using very small, tight brush-strokes in just two colors, brown and white. A female figure in a similar pose, barely sketched in and with its gesture subsequently corrected, is to be seen in the background of the canvas showing *Achilles Plunged into the Styx*.

A variant of this figure appears in the right foreground in the *Allegorical Tomb of Joseph Addison* (Villa Wolkonsky, Rome, Roli 1990, *Il Creti a Palazzo*, p. 50 and fig. 73). The same figure is used again in an unrelated canvas in a private collection (Biagi Maino, awaiting publication).

The girl's head reappears, inclined in an even more melancholy pose, on a sheet in the Pinacoteca Nazionale, Bologna showing studies of three heads, where it is a later reworking of an earlier invention (inv. 1764; Giannattasio in Faietti-Zacchi 1998, pp. 264-65, no. 87).

Bibliography
Zanotti 1739, II, p. 113; Oretti B. 130, c. 162; Zaist 1774, II, p. 127; Zucchini 1934, p. 57; Bologna 1935, p. 32, no. 2; Foratti 1935, pp. 27-28; Zucchini 1938, p. 62; Roli 1959, p. 334; Roli 1967, *Donato Creti*, pp. 87-88, fig. 48; Roli 1977, *Pittura Bolognese 1650 - 1800*, pp. 117-118, no. 53; Roli in Bologna 1979, p. 62, no. 109; Roli 1990, *Il Creti a Palazzo*, p. 50.

about 1715–1721
Oil on canvas
105x175 cm

Enchained Male Nude

Enchained Male Nude may be regarded as one of the most important examples of academic studies in early eighteenth-century Bolognese art, demonstrating in particular the skillful imitation of sculpture. A past, drastic cleaning has made the preparation and weave of the canvas more apparent, revealing as well the way the figure was constructed by progressive corrections to the contours with diluted pigment broadly applied (above all in the right leg and the feet). The surfaces, heightened and smoothed with brush-strokes of ever lighter tones (the same that draw attention to themselves in the landscapes), are lit from no well defined source. These characteristics reflect the atmosphere of the early years of the Accademia Clementina: lessons held in the evening, in artificial light, in rooms specifically arranged. These circumstances may also help explain the analogies with stage design perceptible in Creti's painting.

As in *Sleeping Youth with Winged Putto*, the figure of this painting reveals an intense interest in anatomical structure and musculature, even if, in the present case, the primary interest is in the way light falls on surfaces. The link between painting and sculpture remains strong, as may be observed from the simple detail of the leaf: this is treated with the softness of a naturalistic detail, while its apparent thickness—obtained by means of a few masterly touches of bright highlights and dark finish—suggests a work in stucco.

Bibliography
Zanotti 1739, II, p. 113; Oretti B. 130, c. 162; Zaist 1774, II, p. 127; Zucchini 1934, p. 57; Zucchini 1938, p. 70; Roli 1959, p. 334; Roli 1967, *Donato Creti*, pp. 87-88.

about 1715–1721
Oil on canvas
107x175 cm

Girl Meditating

This image should be read as a perfect and atmospheric "academic" study of the figure and draperies, expressive of a tendency to simplified abstraction that is readily apparent in the metaphysically elegant vase placed upon a step (Roli 1990, p. 50).

Like the *Girl Holding a Flower*, this was one of the revelations of the 1935 exhibition of Bolognese eighteenth-century art. Roberto Longhi may have been thinking of it when, in a discussion of Creti's chiaroscuro, he said that there had returned in this artist, "nearly intact, the elegance of Parmigianino and Primaticcio" (Bologna 1935, p. 30). Rudolph Wittkower sensed a slight neo-Mannerist flavor in this picture, and suggested that it should be dated rather later (Wittkower 1972, pp. 409-410). This work, one of the finest and most original products of Creti's "proto-Neoclassicism," represents the prolongation and persistence over time of Bolognese classicism, anticipating aspects of the late eighteenth century.

The appearance of high-relief suggested by this monochrome is reinforced by the abstract linearity of the background. Upon a yellow-orange ground, the figure has been built up using a method of painting connected with Creti's training in drawing; it recalls work in charcoal and pen. The desired effects are achieved with small brush-strokes in two, or at the most three, tonalities. Volume is obtained by modeling the surface using superimposed brush-strokes of graduated intensity, with brighter strokes for the parts in high-relief and illuminated, darker ones for the shadows and more deeply recessed zones; in some instances, such as the details of the two feet, outlines are emphasized through a sort of illusionistic undercutting. It is above all in the face and the hair that we encounter minute brush-strokes, applied with the extreme tip of a very fine brush, much like the tip of a pen to paper.

Comparisons may be made with both drawings and other paintings by the artist. The female figure in a drawing in the Pinacoteca Nazionale, Bologna is constructed in an analogous manner, especially in the upper part of the garment and the disposition of the draperies (*Venus with an Amorino in a Wood*, inv. 1762; Roli 1967, p. 105, no. 2; Gaeta Bertelà 1972, p. 35, no. 22). This invention also reappears (as does that of the *River God*) in the *Allegorical Tomb of the Marquise of Wharton* (Villa Wolkonsky, Rome), where it is seen atop a tall base (Roli 1967, fig. 72; Roli 1990, p. 50). A sketch for the hand resting upon the cloak has been published Roli (1988, p. 327, fig. 7 and p. 329).

Bibliography
Zanotti 1739, II, p. 113; Oretti B, 130, c. 162; Zaist 1774, II, p. 127; Zucchini 1934, p. 57; Bologna 1935, p. 32, no. 4; Longhi in Bologna 1935, p. 30; Zucchini 1938, p. 64; Roli 1959, p. 334; Roli 1967, *Donato Creti*, pp. 87-88; Roli in Bologna 1979, p. 62, no. 110.

about 1715–1721
Oil on canvas
105x175 cm

River God

Together with the *Girl Meditating*, this is the best preserved of the overdoors. It follows the traditional iconography for a river god: a bearded man, reclining and leaning upon an urn, with his head swathed in marsh grass and his hand grasping an oar. The same figure recurs, with little variation, in *Achilles Plunged into the Styx* and its preparatory oil sketch, now in a private collection in Bologna. The figure is also seen in the foreground of the *Allegorical Tomb of the Marquise of Wharton* (Villa Wolkonsky, Rome), which was painted around 1730. A pen study for the overdoor is in the Held Collection, Binghamton (Binghamton 1970, no. 117). This drawing offers a significant variant: rather than being placed upon the ground, the urn rests on the same rocky base as the river god, who assumes a more forced pose than in the overdoor. The evolution leading to the overdoor, by way of the two canvases showing *Achilles Plunged into the Styx*, is in the increasing distance from the direct study from the model, in a greater overall balance and an ever-more-monumental figure. As elsewhere, in this canvas profiles are softened by means of very thin glazes that counteract any impression of excessive immobility or over-rigid stylization. Calling on his finely honed manual skill in draftsmanship and use of the pen, in this figure Creti demonstrates great command of chiaroscuro technique. The play of light and volume is extraordinarily successful, producing a sort of synthesis of the manners encountered in the *Girl Meditating* and the *Enchained Male Nude*. It is easy to perceive the way in which the work has been developed starting with a division into two principal zones: the one where the rock has been painted, and the landscape. The former has been prepared in paler, the latter in darker tones: in both cases, the preparatory color is highly diluted. Over this preparation there have been built up successive, repeated, very fine layers in similar tones, sometimes broadly applied, sometimes blended with the immediately underlying layer, sometimes painted in very small, tight strokes; Creti frequently adopts a similar procedure. Nothing could be farther from full bodied technique that, in seventeenth-century Bologna, was typical of even such orthodox classicists as Guido Reni and Francesco Albani. What exchanges there may have been between the art of Creti and the "purism" of Marcantonio Franceschini remains to be studied. It is important to emphasize how Creti's particular variety of classicism pursues its ideal of perfection while rejecting the seventeenth-century academic norm based on theoretical principles, the classification of gestures and expressions, and the fusion of the human figure with Nature. Tracing the genesis of Creti's vision step by step helps to clarify the highly personal interpretation of academic concepts characteristic of his painting. In the present case, he arrives at his classically composed form on the basis of a study from the live model which is subsequently liberated through an extraordinary manual dexterity from an overly close adherence to reality. Creti here finds a way of reconciling the academic classicism practiced by the Carracci and their school, based upon their adherence to what Roberto Longhi once famously called an "open window" on visual reality, with the new experimental spirit of the early eighteenth century. Creti thus goes beyond the seventeenth-century phase of theoretical pronouncements to favor a personal aesthetic sensibility employing a consolidated vocabulary of drawing and painting.

Bibliography
Zanotti 1739, II, p. 113; Oretti B. 130, c. 162; Zaist 1774, II, p. 127; Bologna 1935, pp. 324-327; Zucchini 1938 p. 65 n. 7.

about 1715–1721
Oil on canvas
105x175 cm

Nude with a Putto

This canvas and the following one seem to have originated as a pair. They share the reddish hue of the ground and a level of execution which seems to have stopped at a similar point, without having reached the high finish of the preceding overdoors. In these two canvases, as in the *Virtues*, Creti draws upon the memory of old compositions linked to Renaissance inventions; as in the *Enchained Male Nude*, he returns to the study from the model practiced at the beginning of the century by academic painters and sculptors. The creation of a space delineated by a curtain in which the figures and the architectural elements are situated, relates this picture with the type of experimentation that had begun with the tondi of the *Virtues*. The architectural elements encountered here may be considered a variant of the rocky plateaus, delicately draped couches, or pillows that often accompany Creti's figures; they become the instruments of a summary, abstract setting where the precise definition of perspective and space is deliberately avoided. These two overdoors are connected with the *Virtues*, and were probably painted after them.

The figure of a reclining man appears in a drawing in the Albertina, Vienna showing a couple of lovers in the open air (inv. 34892, Birke 1979). The spatial construction of the Vienna drawing closely follows that of the overdoor *River God*, with the oblique division between the rocky zone and the landscape; the female figure in it is a monumental amplification comparable to the *Virtues*. As in the case of *River God*, this chain of inventions helps clarify both Creti's creative methods and the genesis and chronology of the works commissioned by Collina Sbaraglia.

Bibliography
Zanotti 1739, II, p. 113; Oretti B. 130, c. 162; Zaist 1774, II, p. 127; Zucchini 1934, p. 57; Bologna, 1935, p. 32, n. 13; Zucchini 1938, p. 65; Roli 1959, p. 334; Roli 1967, *Donato Creti*, pp. 87-88.

about 1715–1721
Oil on canvas
105x175 cm

Sleeping Youth with Winged Putto

The observations offered a propos of the preceding canvas also hold good for this one, especially the reference to "stage props" arranged to the figures.

A very beautiful preparatory grisaille in oil on paper is now in the Prado, Madrid: instead of the curtain it shows the tall base of a column (Perez Sanchez 1968, no. 74; Roli 1990, *Il Creti a Palazzo*, p. 50 and p. 51, fig. 5). This nude figure may be connected with a drawing of a *Sleeping Endymion* now in the Pinacoteca Nazionale, Bologna. On the back of the latter there appears the inscription "donato chreti 1716" (inv. 1846; on the back appear two studies in sanguine, one of them a study for an arm connected with the *Temperance*).

Endymion is shown lying in the open air in a pose similar to that seen in the present painting, but more relaxed. (Attention is drawn to this analogy in Roli 1967, p. 105, no. 7.) The drawing reflects the same poetics of the idyllic expressed in those connected with the *Sleeping Woman*, the *Seated Woman with a Pheasant*, and the *Nude with a Putto*.

Bibliography
Zanotti 1739, II, p. 113; Oretti B. 130, c. 162; Zaist 1774, II, p. 127; Zucchini 1934, p. 57; Mostra del Settecento bolognese, 1935, pp. 32-33; Zucchini 1938, p. 65; Roli 1959, p. 334; Roli 1967, *Donato Creti*, pp. 87-88; Roli 1990, *Il Creti a Palazzo*, pp. 50-51.

Donato Creti
Seated Woman with a Pheasant
about 1715–1721
tempera on canvas
Collezioni Comunali d'Arte
di Palazzo d'Accursio, Bologna

Donato Creti
Sleeping Woman
about 1715–1721
tempera on canvas
Collezioni Comunali d'Arte
di Palazzo d'Accursio, Bologna

Mercury, Paris and Juno

Two large paintings with life-sized figures

Giovan Pietro Zanotti, 1739

In the two canvases showing *Mercury Giving the Golden Apple to Paris* and *Mercury Bringing the Head of Argus to Juno*, the messenger of the gods has the principal role. As with the overdoors, both pictures are characterized by an "ostentatious, captious, and calligraphic" display of the nude figure.[1] As in the series of Virtues, ancient mythological and allegorical traditions are translated into a natural, clearly structured idiom. However, the intentions underlying the commission for these two pictures is not immediately clear. Although the choice of subjects probably combines various allusions that encapsulate the entire cycle. It has been noted that a common thematic thread links these two works with the cycle of the four *Stories of Achilles*, for the apple that Mercury brings to Paris on Juno's orders is the same one thrown by Discord onto the banquet table at the wedding of Achilles's parents Peleus and Thetis.[2] By giving the apple to Venus, Paris aroused the ire of Juno and precipitated the Trojan war, in which Hector died (an event included in the *Stories of Achilles*).[3] On another level, the god Mercury appears in the monument to Marcello Malpighi painted by Marco Antonio Franceschini[4] in the Archiginnasio, then seat of the University of Bologna. As messenger of the gods, herald of the arts and sciences among men, Mercury figured prominently in the new cultural orientation of the university that begins in the mid-sixteenth-century, under the pontificate of Pius IV. A statue of Mercury touching earth, symbolizing Reason and Truth, was to be placed in the center of the courtyard of the Archiginnasio as a reminder to the students that "wisdom descends from Heaven and is a gift from God, to be sought after with the utmost study and veneration."[5] Mercury is, among other things, the protector of the medical arts.

The allusion to Mercury's spirit of initiative, and to the varied activities over which he presides, was perhaps dictated by the commitment of Creti's patron to the city's cultural life, a commitment connected with the inheritance he had received from Girolamo Sbaraglia.[6] Nor can it be ruled out that the reference to Discord reflects the controversies over that inheritance. In the same way, the idea of memory traditionally linked with Juno and the animal sacred to her, the peacock, probably alludes to the figure of the benefactor.

A recent study of the documents situates the commencement of work on the two pictures in late 1721;[7] the most important stylistic parallel is with a picture of *Jacob Struggling with the Angel* painted for Cardinal Giovan Antonio Davia (1660-1740),[8] now in the Casa del Clero, Bologna. Here, too, we find what Roli has described as "the invisible grid that controls the absolute equilibrium, the studied symmetry of poses, pursued with the same stubborn commitment."

1. Roli 1990, *Il Creti a Palazzo*, p. 52.
2. We may also note that Paris, shown at the center of one of two canvases, was latter to slay Achilles.
3. Biagi Maino 1987, p. 130.
4. The statue, which was to have been executed by Giambologna, was never made; the preparatory bronze model has survived in Bologna's Museo Civico Medievale; cf. Tuttle 1987, p. 84 and Lavin 1992, pp. 17-18.
5. Roli 1990, *Il Creti a Palazzo*, p. 52.
6. Marcon 1990, p. 129; Roli 1990, *Il Creti a Palazzo*, pp. 51-52.
7. Roli 1967, *Donato Creti*, p. 39; Bonfait 1990, pp. 87-88; Roli 1991, p. 225.

about 1721
Oil on canvas
272x166 cm

Mercury Giving the Golden Apple to Paris

None of Creti's pictures illustrates better than this one that characteristic singled out as peculiar to Bolognese painting. The late eighteenth-century historian Luigi Lanzi, who wrote the first coherent history of Italian painting, noted as an ever-present element in Bolognese artistic culture that "method of a true and praiseworthy imitation," that gives rise to the "transmission of pictorial inventions and a concatenation of models". (Lanzi 1789; Mazza in Emiliani 1998 pp. 371 and 381). The figure of Paris expresses a kind of emulation of the ideal beauty and cult of form that constituted the very soul of the painting of Guido Reni, as embodied in his *Samson Victorious* (Pinacoteca Nazionale, Bologna). But Bolognese artistic culture offers other precedents. As Christel Thiem has noted, Creti's canvas incorporates elements of a work by Ludovico Carracci, the *Saint Roch Comforted by an Angel* (San Giacomo Maggiore, Bologna); it is from the latter work that Creti would appear to have derived both the position of Paris's arms and the hunting dog lying at his feet (Thiem 1988-89, p. 497 and p. 494, fig. 86). Creti omits the strongly naturalistic components of Ludovico Carracci's universe—those effects of light and shade, that tendency to linger over details. This thread of visual memory finds intermediate moments of expression in Guido Reni's *David with the Head of Goliath* (Ringling Museum, Sarasota, Florida) and in a more closely related *David* by Burrini (San Sal-

vatore, Bologna). In the church of San Salvatore, Bologna, Creti had drawn upon the latter work in his youth, especially for a terracotta statue of *David* (Liebighaus, Frankfurt: Götz Mohr 1988, pp. 88-92) that has been ascribed to him partly on the basis of a comparison with a *Bacchus*, also attributed to our artist, and quite close to the figure of Paris (Roli 1964; Riccòmini 1965, pp. 71-72, no. 50). Paris, a Trojan hero who was the son of Priam and Hecuba, is shown standing in the foreground, dressed as a shepherd. As befits the pastoral setting, Mercury is portrayed in accordance with the more usual, less rarefied iconography: instead of the broad-brimmed petasus, he wears a winged head-dress; in place of the caduceus—the staff with two intertwined serpents that has come to symbolize his role as the god of health—he carries a simple staff. The double *pentimento* in the figure of Paris—in his torso two different versions of a shoulder bag may be detected—is probably the outcome of the artist's reluctance to mar the purity of the nude. The figure of Mercury, and its relationship with that of Paris, shows less decisiveness and security in its composition. The point of departure is a nude figure analogous to the one appearing in the overdoor showing a *Nude Youth with a Putto*; the pose has thus originally been conceived for a static presentation and the artist seems to have tried to achieve an effect of free movement in air by means of adjustments intended to cor-

rect an imperfect foreshortening and solve the problem of relating Mercury's and Paris's gestures. These adjustments are also probably meant to avoid making the figure stand out too starkly: in particular, to limit the extent to which Mercury's hand breaks through the picture plane. When we compare this picture with its pendant, *Mercury Bringing Juno the Head of Argus*, we observe that in the first work the figure of Mercury is placed at the same height as that of Juno in the other, but without taking on a comparable importance. It may be in order to maintain this hierarchy of importance that the green of Mercury's mantle merges gently into the blue background of the sky, while the hand holding the apple has remained at a level of less than complete finish and the right leg has been scarcely more than sketched in. This leg "fades away" in depth, as an alternative to a conventional foreshortening: it thus remains without the winged feet which are one of Mercury's usual attributes (an attribute, by the way, for which Creti also fails to find a satisfactory solution in the other foot).

Bibliography
Bologna 1935, p. 33, n. 20; Zanotti 1939, II, p. 112; Malvasia-Zanotti 1755, p. 180; De la Lande 1769, in Sorbelli 1973, p. 231; Oretti 1770, B. 130, c. 162; Zaist 1744, II, p. 127; Bassani 1817, p. 20; Zucchini 1934, p. 57; Zucchini 1938, p. 68; Roli 1959, p. 334; Roli 1967, *Donato Creti*, p. 87; Roli 1977, *Pittura Bolognese 1650 - 1800*, p. 29, 117; Thiem 1988 - 1989, p. 535; Roli 1990, *Il Creti a Palazzo*, p. 51-52.

about 1721
Oil on canvas
272x166 cm

Mercury Bringing Juno the Head of Argus

Like its companion, *Mercury Giving the Golden Apple to Paris*, this picture is closely related both in style and, in all probability, chronology to certain of the overdoors, as may be seen both in the degree of definition of the nude figure and in the treatment of the landscape background. The latter harks back to Reni's stylized, abstract horizons (of which an example occurs in the *Samson*). As in the two overdoors with the *Girl Holding a Flower* and the *River God*, the effect of distance is obtained by allowing the pictorial ground to show through as a color. The figure of Juno seated on the cloud is one of those masterpieces at which Creti arrived by following a logical progression that begins with the *Sbaraglia memorial*, where the figures of *Experience* and *Reason* already reveal a powerful aspiration towards an ideal of pure, chilly, sophisticatedly intellectual formal beauty (Roli 1967; Biagi Maino 1987, p. 135). Over the ensuing years, Creti followed the twists and turns of a subtle dialectic between naturalism and idealism that marked the crucial period of the execution of the *Virtues* and led to a recovery of that sensitivity and softness found in the extremely pure, female nude in the *Achilles Entrusted to Chiron*. The details of this development in Creti's study of the female figure can only be clarified through further investigation of the artist's numerous drawings: their chronology and their sources, some recent and some going back to hard-to-recognize classical statuary and the full-blown Venetian classicism of the second decade of the sixteenth century.

To turn to questions of iconography, the slaying of the shepherd Argus constitutes one of the best known stories of Mercury. As told by Ovid in the *Metamorphoses* (I, 583 ff.), the myth is connected with Jupiter's love for the nymph Io. In order to hide the latter from the suspicious Juno, his wife, Jupiter transformed the nymph into a splendid heifer and denied having any interest in her. The shrewd Juno, however, entrusted Io to the custody of the shepherd Argus, half of whose hundred eyes were always open. Jupiter ordered Mercury to free Io, and the messenger of the gods lulled Argus's open eyes to sleep, and then slew him (Grimal 1951, ed. 1996, p. 207 and p. 231; Graves 1958, ed. 1967, p. 158). In everlasting memory of Argus, Juno turned the latter's eyes into the ornaments on the feathers of her sacred animal, the peacock. For this reason, the figure of Juno with her peacock is associated with the idea of memory (Graves 1958, ed. 1967, p. 158; Seznec 1980, ed. 1990, fig. 30). A figure of "shining" Argus appears on the frontispiece of an astronomical book published in Bologna in the mid-seventeenth century (Battistini 1988, p. 161).

A study for the figure of Mercury is found on the sheet of charcoal and sanguine drawings in the Janos Scholz Collection in the Pierpont Morgan Library, New York (Roli 1990, pp. 50-51). A sketch was shown at the exhibition of eighteenth-century Bolognese art held in Bologna in 1935. (Bologna 1935, p. 38, no. 1).

Bibliography
Bologna 1935, p. 33, Zanotti 1939, II, p. 112; Malvasia-Zanotti 1755, p. 180; De la Lande 1769, in Sorbelli 1973, p. 231; Oretti 1770, B. 130, c. 162; Zaist, 1744, II, p. 127; Zucchini 1934, p. 57; Bologna 1935, p. 33, no. 14; Zucchini 1938, p. 66; Roli 1959, p. 334; Roli 1967, *Donato Creti*, p. 87 no. 19, fig. 59; Roli 1977, *Pittura Bolognese 1650 - 1800*; p. 29, 117; Roli in Bologna 1979, p. 61; Roli 1990, *Il Creti a Palazzo*, pp. 51-52.

post. 1713
Oil on canvas
122x91 cm

A detail from the Sbaraglia memorial Two Children Playing

The canvas of two children at play does not belong to the cycle commissioned by Marco Antonio Sbaraglia. The work, which became the property of city of Bologna in the nineteenth century, should in all probability be identified with a picture of "two putti embracing, drawn from life" recorded in an inventory in Palazzo Fava (Campori 1870; Roli 1967, p. 87, no. 14). It is a reworking of a detail from the destroyed *memorial* to Girolamo Sbaraglia (formerly Palazzo dell'Archiginnasio, 1713), a project that inaugurated one of Creti's most felicitous creative periods. In the *memorial*, the two figures allude to Experience and Reason and point out to the viewer a large portrait medallion of the Bolognese physician executed in bronze by Giuseppe Mazza, a brilliant and refined sculptor who was Creti's contemporary (Biagi Maino, 1987, p. 135). Below, two genii, were shown lifting a laurel wreath. In the picture exhibited here the invention takes on a life of its own, free from any al-

legorical or celebratory references. The inspiration provided by Guido Reni is apparent in the effects of light and anatomical rendering, which recall the earlier painter's *Saint Sebastian* (Palazzo Rosso, Genoa; Bologna 1988, p. 66, no. 23), while the pursuit of a naturalistic dimension owes much to Simone Cantarini; nor is there lacking an obeisance to the grace of Parmigianino (Mazza in Emiliani, 1997, p. 381). In this work, as in others by Creti, much attention has been devoted to stage-like artifice, as may be seen in the fanciful handling of the fabrics against which the figures are posed and in the way the space is linked to the picture plain by means of a curtain. The curvaceous shadow of the fabric touches the upper part of the standing child, where extensive, apparently unfinished passages, accentuate the effectiveness of the penumbra. In the lower part of the canvas the artist displays a piece of pure painting, expressed in the play of light, the optical fragmentation of

the draperies, and the rapid, busy brushstrokes: if seen out of context, this passage could easily be taken for the work of a later epoch. Here the artist's manner of tracing lines and visible marks with his brush is quite unusual; the strokes are on a larger scale than usual, as though he wished to provide an eloquent demonstration of his technique and skill. This aspect would be more easily explainable if it could be proven that this work is indeed the one from Palazzo Fava, perhaps commissioned by the count himself. There also exists another partial replica of the *Sbaraglia memorial*: the splendid canvas representing *Experience* now in a private collection in Bologna (Roli 1967, pp. 34 and 91; Biagi 1987, p. 135).

Bibliography
Zucchini 1934, p. 62; Bologna 1935, p. 34 no. 18; Zucchini 1938, p. 64; Roli 1959, p. 340; Roli 1967, *Donato Creti*, p. 87, no. 14, fig. 33; Mazza in Emiliani 1997, p. 381.

Bibliography

Note
The bibliography is divided into two sections: the first one refers specifically to Donato Creti, the second one is more general.

Abbate, V. *"Donato Creti: un dipinto per Palermo"*, in *Le arti in Sicilia nel Settecento. Studi in memoria di Maria Accascina*, Palermo, 1986.

Abbate, V. *"Palermo 1700: i contatti con Bologna e la committenza del Marchese di Regolamici"*, in *Barocco Mediterraneo: Sicilia, Lecce, Sardegna, Spagna. Corso Internazionale di Alta Cultura* (22 October - 7 November 1987), Rome, 1992, pp. 295-328.

Agnelli, J. *Galleria di pittura dell'E.mo e R.mo Principe Signor Card. Tommaso Ruffo vescovo di Palestrina e di Ferrara* (Rime e prose), Ferrara, 1734.

Alcsuti, K. *"Donato Creti"*, in *Il Comune di Bologna*, September 1932, pp. 17-32.

Arfelli, A. *"Bologna perlustrata"* by Paolo Masini Antonio and l'*"Aggiunta"*, 1690, in *"L'Archiginnasio"*, LII, 1957, pp. 186-203.

Bacchi, A. Benati, D. *La collezione di dipinti attraverso cinque schede*, in Ottani Cavina A. ed., *Palazzo Poggi da dimora aristocratica a sede dell'Università di Bologna*, Bologna, 1988, pp. 138-150.

Bassani, P. *Guida agli amatori delle Belle Arti, Architettura, Pittura e Scultura, per la città di Bologna*, vol. I, p. II, Bologna, 1817.

Bean, J. *17th Century Italian Drawings in the Metropolitan Museum of Art*, New York, 1979.

Benati, D. in *Sacro e Profano nell'arte emiliana da Passerotti a Gandolfi*, Bologna, 1995, pp. 56-57.

Bernardini, C. in *Collezioni Comunali d'Arte. L'Appartamento del Legato in Palazzo d'Accursio*, Bologna, 1989.

Bernardini, C. *Le Collezioni Comunali d'Arte*, in *Storia illustrata di Bologna*, vol. III, Bologna, 1989, pp. 181-200.

Biagi Maino, D. *La gratitudine e la memoria. I monumenti affrescati di età barocca*, in Roversi G. ed. L'Archiginnasio. *Il Palazzo, l'Università, la Biblioteca*, Bologna, 1987, pp. 113-143.

Biagi Maino, D. *Prolegomeni al classicismo accademico tra Bologna e Roma*, in *La pittura romana dal protoneoclassicismo al Neoclassicismo e le sue diramazioni nell'area italiana* (Acts of the Convention, Raito-Ravello, Giugno 1977), currently in course of pubblication.

Bianconi, G. *Guida del forestiere per la città di Bologna*, Bologna, 1820.

Binghamton 1970, *Drawings from the Held Collection*, University Art Gallery of Binghamton (exhibition catalogue), Binghamton 1970.

Birke, V. *"Neue Zeichnungen Donato Cretis"*, in *Wiener Jahrbuch für Kunstgeschichte*, Vienna, 1979, pp. 49-57

Bologna 1935, *Mostra del Settecento bolognese* (exhibition catalogue), Bologna, 1935.

Bologna 1979, *L'Arte del Settecento emiliano. La pittura, l'Accademia Clementina* (Catalogue, 10th Biennale d'Arte Antica), Bologna, 1979.

Bologna 1988, *Alla scoperta del Barocco italiano. La collezione Denis Mahon* (exhibition catalogue, Finaldi G. and Kitson M. ed.), Bologna, 1988.

Bologna 1990, *Giuseppe Maria Crespi 1665-1747* (exhibition catalogue, Emiliani A. and Rave A.B. ed.), Bologna, 1990. (Mazza A., *Dall'eredità di Guido Reni a Giuseppe Maria Crespi. Cinquant'anni di pittura a Bologna*, pp. XLIII-LXII; Mazza A. *I "turgidi floridi affreschi"* in Palazzo Pepoli, pp. CCVII-CCXVI)

Bonfait, O. *"Il valore della pittura. L'economia del mecenatismo di Pompeo Aldrovandi"*, in *Arte a Bologna*. Bollettino dei Musei Civici d'Arte antica, no. 1, 1990, pp. 83-94.

Brizzi, G.P. *"I collegi religiosi. La Compagnia di Gesù"*, in *Le sedi della Cultura nell'Emilia Romagna. I secoli moderni. Le Istituzioni e il pensiero*, Milan, 1987, pp. 111-125.

Campori, G. *Raccolta di cataloghi ed inventari inediti di quadri, statue, disegni, Bronzi... dal secolo XV al secolo XIX*, Modena, 1870, pp. 602-615.

Caracciolo, M.T. *"Dessins du Settecento Bolonais au Musée des arts décoratifs de Lyon: Oeuvres inédites ou nouvellement attribuées"*, in *Revue du Louvre*, October 1993, pp. 25-44.

Casali Pedrielli, C. *Vittorio Maria Bigari. Affreschi, dipinti disegni*, Bologna, 1991.

Ceschi Lavagetto, P. in *Arte e Pietà. I patrimoni culturali delle Opere Pie nella Provincia di Piacenza* (exhibition catalogue, Piacenza), Bologna, 1981.

Chicago 1970, *Painting in Italy in the Eighteenth Century: Rococo to Romanticism* (exhibition catalogue), Chicago 1970.

Colombo, E. *"La biblioteca negata. Marcantonio Collina Sbaraglia e i suoi tentativi di fondar una "pubblica libreria" a Bologna nei primi decenni del '700"*, in *Il Carrobbio*, no. IX, 1983, pp. 107-129.

Crespi, L. *Vite de' pittori bolognesi non descritte nella Felsina pittrice*, Rome, 1769.

Emiliani, A. ed. *Simone Cantarini detto il Pesarese 1612-1648* (exhibition catalogue, Bologna), Milan 1997, (Ambrosini Massari, A.M. *Leggiadria e grazioso dispregio di que' bei segni*, pp. 304-357; Mazza A. *"Il metodo d'una vera e lodevole imitazione"*. *La fortuna di Simone Cantarini nella pittura bolognese della seconda metà del Seicento e del primo Settecento*, pp. 359-396.)

Farneti, F. *"I Maestri dell'Accademia Clementina"* (1710-1803), in *Accademia Clementina. Atti e Memorie*, no. 23, 1988, pp. 93-102.

Foratti, A. *"La mostra del Settecento Bolognese"*, in *Bologna*, XXII, no. 6, June 1935, pp. 21-32.

Gaeta Bertelà, G. and Ferrara S. ed., *Incisori bolognesi ed emiliani del sec. XVIII*, Bologna, 1974.

Gaeta Bertelà, G. *Artisti italiani dal XVI al XIX secolo. Mostra di 200 disegni* (exhibition catalogue), Bologna, 1976.

Gatti, G. *Descrizione delle più rare cose di Bologna*, Bologna, 1803.

Götz Mohr, B. *"Italien, Frankreich Niederlande, 1500-1800"* Liebighaus-Museum Alter Plastik, *Nachantike klein plastische Bildwerke*, vol. II, Melsungen, 1988.

Grandi, R. *Bernardo Minozzi, Carlo Lodi*, Musei Civici d'Arte Antica, "*Ospiti 5*", Bologna, 1997.

Grandi, R. "*Un Creti a metà (o qualcosa d'altro)*", in *Arte a Bologna*. Bollettino dei Musei Civici d'Arte antica, no. 1, 1990, pp. 131-132.

Gualandi, M. *Tre giorni in Bologna*, Bologna, 1850.

Haskell, F. *Patron and Painters*, italian trad. *Mecenati e Pittori*, Florence, 1966.

Johns, C.M.S. "*Art and Science in Eighteenth Century Bologna: Donato Creti's Astronomical Landscape Paintings*", in *Zeitschrift für Kunstgeschichte*, IV 1992, pp. 578-589.

Johns, C.M.S. *Papal Art and Cultural Politics. Rome in The Age of Clement XI*, Cambridge, 1993.

Johnston, C. "*Donato Creti par R. Roli*", in *L'oeil*, no. 168, 1968.

Kaufmann, O. and Schlagete, F. *L'Amour de l'art; le goût de deux amateurs pour le baroque italien* (exhibition catalogue), Strasburg, 1987.

Lanzi, L. *Storia pittorica dell'Italia dal Risorgimento delle Belle Arti fin presso la fine del XVIII secolo*, vol. V, Bassano, 1789, Capucci M. ed., vol. III, Florence, 1974.

Lloyd, C. "*Four Drawings by Donato Creti in the Guise Collection*", in *The Burlington Magazine*, no. 111, 1969, pp. 374-377.

Longhi, R. "*Momenti della pittura bolognese*", in *L'Archiginnasio*, no. XXX, 1935, republished in *Lavori in Valpadana*, Florence, 1973, pp. 189-205.

Macandrew, H. *Ashmolean Museum Oxford: Catalogue of the Collection of Drawings. III. Italian School*, Supplement, Oxford, 1980.

Manning, R.L. ed. *Baroque Painters of Bologna* (exhibition catalogue, Finch College), New York, 1962.

Marcon, G. "*Un inedito su Donato Creti. Il ciclo 'Collina Sbaraglia' in un documento dell'Archivio di Stato di Bologna*", in *Arte a Bologna*. Bollettino dei Musei Civici d'Arte Antica, no. 1, 1990, pp. 127-130.

Marqués, M. "*Les Collections de dessins italiens en Espagne*", in *Revue de l'Art*, 1985, no. 70, pp. 83-90.

Mauceri, E. "*Nel Settecento bolognese. Donato Creti*", in *Il Comune di Bologna*, November 1930.

Mazza, A. *Donato Creti*, in Bentini J. and Mazza A. ed. *Disegni emiliani del Sei-Settecento. I grandi cicli di affreschi*, Modena, 1990, pp. 230-237 (with bibliography).

Mazza, A. "*Ercole e Cerbero. Un affresco del Creti diciassettenne in Palazzo Fava ed altre opere giovanili*", in *Arte a Bologna*. Bollettino dei Musei Civici d'Arte antica, no. 2, 1992, pp. 97-123.

Mazza, A. "*Le pale d'altare e la quadreria della sagrestia. Pittura bolognese tra classicismo ed accademia*", in *La cattedrale di San Pietro in Bologna*, Terra R. ed., Bologna, 1997, pp. 112-131.

Mazza A. "*Per gli inizi di Donato Creti in Palazzo Fava*", in *Arte a Bologna*. Bollettino dei Musei Civici di Arte Antica, no. 5, currently in course of publication.

Miller, D. G. "*Donato Creti*", in *The Burlington Magazine*, May 1969, pp. 306-307.

Miller, D.C. item "*Creti Donato*", in *Dizionario biografico degli italiani*, vol. 30, Rome, 1984, pp. 749-752.

Miller, D.C. *Marcantonio Franceschini and the Liechtensteins Prince Johann Adam Andreas and the Decoration of the Liechtenstein Garden Palace at Rossau-Vienna*, Cambridge, 1991, pp. 212-28.

Montefusco Bignozzi, F. "*La colonia Renia e le Arti figurative*", in *La Colonia Renia: profilo documentario e critico dell'Arcadia bolognese, II: momenti e problemi*, (M. Saccenti ed.), Modena, 1988, pp. 361-424.

Noè, E. "*Ferdinand de Saint-Urbain, medaglista bolognese*", in *La medaglia*, no. 22, 1987, pp. 62-87.

Oretti, M. *Notizie de' Professori del disegno... bolognesi e di forestieri di sua scuola*, (1770) Bologna, Biblioteca Comunale dell'Archiginnasio, ms. B. 130, (vol. VIII).

Orlandi, P.A. *Abecedario pittorico*, Bologna, 1704.

Ottani Cavina, A. and Roli, A. *Storia dell'Accademia Clementina di Bologna. Commentario all'opera di G. P. Zanotti*, Bologna, 1977.

Paris 1960, *La peinture italienne au XVIII siècle* (exhibition catalogue), Paris, 1960.

Parker, R.T. *Catalogue of the collection of drawings in the Ashmolean Museum*, II, Oxford, 1956.

Perini, G. "*Donato Creti inconsueto*", in *Arte a Bologna*. Bollettino dei Musei Civici d'Arte antica, no. 1, 1990, pp. 59-72.

Pescarmona, D. ed. *Disegni emiliani dei secoli XVII-XVIII della Pinacoteca di Brera* (exhibition catalogue), Milan, 1995, (Roli R. *Itinerario del disegno bolognese di età barocca*, pp. 17-29 and *Donato Creti*, pp. 166-173, no. 52-55).

Riccòmini, E. "*Saggio introduttivo*", in *L'Arte del Settecento emiliano. La pittura, l'Accademia Clementina* (catalogue, 10th Biennale d'Arte Antica), Bologna, 1979, pp. XXIX-XLIV.

Riccòmini E. *Mostra della scultura bolognese del Settecento* (exhibition catalogue), Bologna, 1965, pp. 25-54 and 70-72.

Riccòmini, E. *Pittura italiana del Settecento* (exhibition catalogue, Leningrad, Moscow, Warsaw), Bologna, 1974.

Riccòmini, M. "*A Rediscovered Bozzetto by Donato Creti*", in *The Burlington Magazine*, no. 131, 1989, pp. 420-421.

Riccòmini, M. "*Aggiunte al Creti*", in *Accademia Clementina. Atti e memorie*, no. 24, n.s., Bologna, 1989, pp. 61-63.

Roli, R. "*Donato Creti (1671-1749)*", in *Arte Antica e Moderna*, no. 7, July -September 1959, pp. 328-341.

Roli, R. "*I disegni di Donato Creti agli Uffizi*", in *Bollettino d'Arte*, XLVII, 1962, pp. 241-250.

Roli, R. "*Dipinti inediti di Donato Creti*", in *Arte Antica e Moderna*, no. 23, 1963, pp. 247-253.

Roli, R. "*Donato Creti: un 'Bacco' in terracotta*", in *Arte Antica e Moderna*, no. 25, 1964, pp. 101-102.

Roli, R. *Donato Creti*, Milan, 1967.

Roli, R. *"Peintures de Donato Creti dans les Musées de France"*, in *La Revue du Louvre*, 1967, nos. 4-5, pp. 249-255.

Roli, R. *Donato Creti. 46 disegni inediti*, Bologna, 1973.

Roli, R. *"Drawings by Donato Creti: Notes for a Chronology"*, in *Master Drawings*, XI, no. 1, 1973, pp. 25-32.

Roli, R. *"Giovan Pietro Zanotti e la Storia dell'Accademia Clementina"*, in Ottani Cavina A. and Roli R., *Storia dell'Accademia Clementina di Bologna. Commentario all'opera di G.P. Zanotti*, Bologna, 1977.

Roli, R. *"Classicismo e barocchetto all'interno della situazione bolognese 'clementina', Donato Creti"*, in *L'Arte del Settecento emiliano. La pittura, l'Accademia Clementina* (catalogue, 10th Biennale d'Arte Antica), Bologna, 1979, pp. 42-46, 55-77.

Roli, R. and Sestieri, G. *I disegni italiani del Settecento. Scuole piemontese, lombarda, genovese, bolognese, toscana, romana e napoletana*, Treviso, 1981.

Roli, R. *La pittura del Sei e Settecento*, in *Storia illustrata di Bologna*, vol. III, Bologna, 1988, pp. 261-280.

Roli, R. *"Le scene astronomiche di Donato Creti"*, in A. Ottani Cavina ed., *Palazzo Poggi da dimora aristocratica a sede dell'Università di Bologna*, Bologna 1988, pp. 151-156.

Roli, R. *"Una insolita Veronica di Donato Creti e altre aggiunte"*, in *Scritti di storia dell'arte in onore di Raffaello Causa*, Naples, 1988, pp. 325-330.

Roli, R. *"La pittura in Emila Romagna nella prima metà del Settecento"*, in *La pittura in Italia. Il Settecento*, Milan, 1989, vol. I pp. 252-275 and vol. II, pp. 685-686 (with bibliography).

Roli, R. *"Mostra di disegni bolognesi del Museo di Budapest"*, in *Paragone*, 40, 1989, n. 473, pp. 94-98.

Roli, R. *"Il Creti a Palazzo: il lascito Collina Sbaraglia al Senato di Bologna (1744)"*, in *Arte a Bologna*. Bollettino dei Musei Civici d'Arte Antica, no. 1, 1990, pp. 47-57.

Roli, R. *"La pittura in Emilia Romagna nella prima metà del Settecento"* and *"Donato Creti"*, in *La pittura in Italia, Il Settecento*, Milan, 1990, vol. I, pp. 252-275, vol. II, pp. 658-686.

Roli, R. *"Ragguagli sulla prima opera in pubblico di Donato Creti"*, in *Paragone*, XLI, no. 483, May 1990, pp. 129-135.

Roli, R. *"Donato Creti"*, in D. Benati ed., *Disegni emiliani del Sei-Settecento. Come nascono i dipinti*, Bologna, 1991, pp. 254-263 (with bibliography).

Romano, G. *Studi sul paesaggio*, Turin, 1978.

Rosenberg, P. *Musée du Louvre. Catalogue de la donation Kaufmann et François Schlageter au Département des Peintures*, Paris, 1984.

Ruggeri, U. *"Nuovi disegni di Donato Creti"*, in *Bollettino dei Musei Ferraresi*, no. 4, 1974, pp. 19-35.

Sandri, M. *"Settecento bolognese a Palazzo d'Accursio"*, no. 7, Bologna, July 1935, pp. 4-10.

Serra, L. *"Le mostre d'arte di Rimini, Parma e Bologna"*, in *Bollettino d'Arte*, XXIX, October 1935, pp. 177-198.

Sorbelli, A. *Bologna negli scrittori stranieri*, Bologna, 1927-1933, republished Bologna, 1973.

Strocchi, M.L., Luigi Crespi ed., *Vite de' Pittori bolognesi non descritte nella Felsina Pittrice, indici ragionati*, Florence, 1986.

Thiem, C. *"Neubestimmte italienische Zeichnungen in der Graphischen Sammlung der Staatsgalerie Stuttgart"*, in *Jahrbuch des Staatlichen Kunstsammlungen in Baden Württenberg*, no. 6, 1969, pp. 189-212.

Thiem, C. *Disegni di artisti bolognesi dal Seicento all'Ottocento delle Collezioni Schloss Fachsenfeld e della Graphische Sammlung Staatsgalerie Stuttgart* (exhibition catalogue), Bologna, 1983.

Thiem, C. *"Das Erbe Guido Renis in Bologna und Emilia Romagna"*, in *Guido Reni und Europa. Ruhm und Nachruhm*, (catalogue edited by Schifferer S.E., Emiliani A. and Schleier E.), Frankfurt - Bologna 1988-89, pp. 489-497, 535, D14.

Volpe, C. *"Lorenzo Pasinelli"*, in *Maestri della pittura del Seicento emiliano* (exhibition catalogue), Bologna, 1959, pp. 160-170.

Voss, H. *"Donato Creti"*, in Thieme U. and Becker V. *Allgemeines Lexicon der bildenden Künstler*, VIII, Leipzig 1913, pp. 100-102.

Wildenstein, D. *"Les tableaux italiens dans les catalogues de ventes parisiennes du XVIIIème siècle"*, in *Gazette des Beaux Arts*, July-August, 1982.

Wittkower, R. *Art and Architecture in Italy: 1600 to 1750*, Harmondsworth 1958, Italian edition, *Arte e architettura in Italia. 1600-1750*, Turin, 1972, pp. 409-410.

Zaist, G.B. *Notizie istoriche de' pittori, scultori e architetti cremonesi*, II, Cremona, 1774.

Zanotti, G.P. *Nuovo fregio di gloria a Felsina sempre pittrice nella vita di Lorenzo Pasinelli*, Bologna, 1703.

Zanotti, G.P. *Storia dell'Accademia Clementina di Bologna aggregata all'Istituto delle Scienze e dell'Arti*, Bologna, 1739, (two volumes).

Zucchini, G. *"Quadri inediti di Donato Creti"*, in *Il Comune di Bologna*, October 1933.

Zucchini, G. *"Opere d'Arte inedite"*, III, in *Il Comune di Bologna*, XXI, no. 10, October 1934, pp. 47-63.

Zucchini, G. *"Collezioni Comunali d'Arte"*, Bologna, October-November 1936, pp. 19-22.

Zucchini, G. *Catalogo delle Collezioni Comunali d'Arte di Bologna*, Bologna, 1938.

General Bibliography

Angeleri, E. *Origini dell'Accademia Clementina*, in *Atti e memorie della Accademia Clementina di Bologna*, XVIII, Bologna, 1985, pp. 41-63.

Angeleri, E. *L'Accademia Clementina di Bologna: struttura e funzioni*, in *Atti e Memorie dell'Accademia Clementina di Bologna*, XIX, Bologna, 1986, pp. 63-109.

Balsamo, L. *"Le biblioteche dei Gesuiti"*, in Brizzi G.P. and Matteucci A.M. ed., *Dall'isola alla città. I Gesuiti a Bologna*, Bologna, 1988, pp. 183-192.

Battistini, A. *"La cultura scientifica nel collegio bolognese"*, in Brizzi G.P. and Matteucci A.M. ed., *Dall'isola alla città. I Gesuiti a Bologna*, Bologna, 1988, pp. 157-169.

Benassi, S. *L'Accademia Clementina. La funzione pubblica. L'ideologia estetica*, Bologna, 1988.

Biagi Maino, D. *Gaetano Gandolfi*, Turin, 1995, pp. 411-412, no. 258.

Bologna, 1962, *L'ideale classico del Seicento in Italia e la pittura di paesaggio* (catalogue, 5th Biennale d'Arte Antica), Bologna, 1962.

Bologna, 1979, *I Materiali dell'Istituto delle Scienze* (exhibition catalogue), Bologna, 1979.

Bologna, 1984, *Bologna 1584. Gli esordi dei Carracci e gli affreschi di Palazzo Fava* (ex-hibition catalogue), Bologna, 1984.

Bologna, 1988, *Guido Reni 1575-1642* (exhibition catalogue, Bologna-Los Angeles, Forth Worth), Bologna, 1988.

Bologna, 1990, *Giuseppe Maria Crespi 1665-1747* (exhibition catalogue, Emiliani V. and Rave A.B. ed.), Bologna, 1990; (Riccòmini E. *"Gli inizi di Giuseppe Maria Crespi: 'Una maniera affatto nuova, tratta però da lunghi studi'"*, pp. LXXXI-IC; Rave A.B. *"Giuseppe Maria Crespi, pittore tra poesia e musica"*, pp. CLXV-CLXXXIII; Boschloo A.A.W. *"Crespi e l'Accademia Clementina"*, pp. CLXXXV, CXCII; Perini G. *"Letteratura artistica e società a Bologna"*, pp. CXCIII-CCVI).

Bologna 1994, *Frammenti di un museo disperso. Il collezionista Agostino Sieri Pepoli e la ricostruzione della sua raccolta bolognese di stampe e disegni*, (ed. by Roncuzzi Roversi Monaco V. and Saccone S.), Bologna 1994

Boschloo, A.W.A. *L'Accademia Clementina e la preoccupazione del passato*, Bologna, 1989.

Cammarota, G.P. *Le origini della Pinacoteca Nazionale di Bologna*, Bologna, 1997.

Cavazza, M. *"Le camere dell'Istituto delle Scienze"*, in *I luoghi del conoscere*, Bologna, 1988, p. 33-43.

Cavazza, M. *Settecento inquieto. Alle origini dell'Istituto delle Scienze di Bologna*, Bologna, 1990.

Colombo, E. *Un progetto mancato nel Settecento: la biblioteca pubblica all'Archiginnasio*, in *L'Archiginnasio*, vol. I, Bologna, 1987, pp. 251-267.

Emiliani, A. *"Introduzione"*, in *Le Collezioni d'Arte della Cassa di Risparmio in Bologna. I dipinti*, Bologna, 1972, pp. 7-36.

Fantuzzi, G. *Notizie degli scrittori bolognesi*, VII, Bologna, 1789.

Farinelli, F. *"Il filosofo e la città: Luigi Ferdinando Marsigli e l'Istituto delle Scienze"*, in *La città del sapere*, Bologna, 1987, pp. 54-75.

Farinelli, F. *"La camera di geografia e nautica"*, in *I laboratori storici dell'Università di Bologna*, in *I luoghi del conoscere*, Bologna, 1988, pp. 73-77.

Frabetti, A. *"Il teatro anatomico dell'Archiginnasio, tra forma simbolica e architettura di servizio"*, in *L'Archiginnasio*, vol. I, Bologna, 1987, pp. 201-218.

Gentili, C. *"L'Accademia delle Scienze"*, in *I luoghi del conoscere*, Bologna, 1988, pp. 45-56.

Gentili, C. *"Musei Scientifici a Bologna tra Cinquecento e Settecento"*, in *I Musei* (*"Capire l'Italia"*), Milan, 1980, pp. 229-233.

Giacomelli, A. *"La dinamica della nobiltà bolognese nel XVIII secolo"*, in *Famiglie senatorie e istituzioni cittadine a Bologna nel Settecento*, acts of the first convention, Bologna, 1980, pp. 55-112.

Grandi, R. *"Il civico Medievale, formazione e vicende"*, in *Introduzione al Museo Civico Medievale. Palazzo Ghisilardi-Fava*, Bologna, 1985, pp. 7-17.

Graves, R. *Greek Myths*, London, 1958, French edition *Les mythes grecs*, Paris, 1967.

Grimal, P. *Dictionnaire de la Mythologie Grecque et Romaine*, Paris, 1951, republished in Paris, 1996.

Gualandi, G. *"Il Museo delle antichità"*, in *I luoghi del conoscere*, Bologna, 1988, pp. 115-122.

Holt, E. A *Documentary History of Art*, Princeton, 1974, Italian edition *Storia documentaria dell'arte*, Milan, 1977.

Lavin, I. *"Bologna è una grande intrecciatura di eresie: il Nettuno del Giambologna al crocevia"*, in Perini G. ed. *Il luogo e il ruolo della città di Bologna tra Europa continentale e mediterranea* (acts of the convention C.I.H.A., 1990), Bologna, 1992, pp. 7-30.

Lenzi, D. *"Le trasformazioni settecentesche: l'Istituto delle Scienze e delle Arti"*, in Ottani Cavina A. ed. *Palazzo Poggi da dimora aristocratica a sede dell'Università di Bologna*, Bologna, 1988, pp. 58-78.

Lovarini, E. *"Luigi Ferdinando Marsigli e l'Accademia Clementina"*, in *Atti e memorie della Reale Accademia Clementina di Bologna*, II, Bologna, 1937, pp. 11-19.

Malvasia, C.C. *Felsina Pittrice. Vite de' pittori bolognesi*, Bologna, 1678 (edited by Zanotti G., Bologna, 1841).

Maylender, M, *Storia delle Accademie d'Italia*, vol. I, Bologna, 1929.

Ottani Cavina, A. *"Le sale affrescate da Nicolò dell'Abate"*, in Ottani Cavina A. ed. *Palazzo Poggi da dimora aristocratica a sede dell'Università di Bologna*, Bologna, 1988, pp. 98-122.

Pelliccioni, A. *"La Mostra di Venezia e la pittura bolognese del Settecento"*, in *Il Comune di Bologna*, September 1929, pp. 63-64.

Pérez Sanchez, A. *I grandi disegni italiani nelle collezioni di Madrid*, Milano, 1978.

Photo Credits

Perini, G. *"La storiografia artistica a Bologna e il collezionismo privato"*, in *Annali della Scuola Normale Superiore di Pisa*, XI, 1981, no. 1, pp. 182-243.

Provenzal, D. *I riformatori della bella letteratura italiana. Eustachio Manfredi, Giampietro Zanotti, Fernand'Antonio Ghedini, Francesco Maria Zanotti. Studio di storia letteraria bolognese del sec. XVIII*, Rocca San Casciano, 1900.

Raimondi, E. *"Settecento bolognese: antichi e moderni"*, in *Padre Martini. Musica e cultura nel Settecento europeo*, Florence 1987, republished in *I lumi e l'erudizione. Saggi sul Settecento italiano*, Milan, 1989, pp. 143-159.

Riccòmini, E. *Ordine e vaghezza. La scultura in Emilia nell'età barocca*, Bologna, 1972.

Riccòmini, E. *Vaghezza e furore. La scultura del Settecento in Emilia*, Bologna, 1977.

Ripa, C. *Iconologia overo descrittione di diverse immagini cavate dall'antichità, e di propria inventione....* , Rome, 1603.

Roli, R. *Pittura bolognese 1650-1800. Dal Cignani ai Gandolfi*, Bologna, 1977.

Roli, R. *"La pittura del secondo Seicento in Emilia"*, in *La pittura in Italia, il Seicento*, Milan, 1989, vol. I, pp. 248-278.

Tuttle, R. *"Il Palazzo dell'Archiginnasio in una relazione inedita di Pier Donato Cesi al Cardinale Carlo Borromeo"*, in *L'Archiginnasio*, vol. I, Bologna, 1987, pp. 65-85.

Zamboni, S. *"L'Accademia Clementina"*, in *L'Arte del Settecento emiliano. La pittura, l'Accademia Clementina* (catalogue, 10th Biennale d'Arte antica), Bologna, 1979, pp. 211-227.

Zamboni, S. *"L'Accademia Clementina"*, in *I luoghi del conoscere*, Bologna, 1988, pp. 115-135.

A view of the Galleria Vidoniana, Bologna

Printed on St. Michael's Day
by Milanostampa Spa
Farigliano, Italy